So Much More

The Story of Parental Care Ministries

By Patrick Butler

For more information please contact:

Parental Care Ministries USA
PO BOX 131166, Tyler, Tx 75713-1166

(903) 526-0499

www.pcmonline.org

100% of the profits of this book will
go to the children of PCM.

CONTENTS

Acknowledgements 4

Introduction 5

1. Building Blocks of Flesh 7

2. Christmas Card 10

3. So Much More 12

4. Parental Care Ministries..15

5. Misery in Mozambique 18

6. Message in a Magazine...21

7. Battling Bitterness...25

8. Near Spiritual Destruction 28

9. Hirelings...34

10. Uganda: The Pearl Tarnished...38

11. Turning Around..41

12. Divine Encounter...43

13. Don't Go Back...46

14. Breakdown 49

15. Meeting in Mbarara..52

16. "You're the One" 56

17. Deception 62

18. All Things Are Possible 66

19. PCM Purpose 71

20. Katyazo Paradise 76

21. The Road to Rwemikoma 80

22. The Crucible of Rejection 84

23. The "Most of These" 86

24. Epilogue: A Revelation 91

25. How He Did It: A Conversation with Mark Barret....................96

ACKNOWLEDGEMENTS

This book was written as a result of an intersection between my two best friends, Monica "Kiconco" Barret and Pastor Emmanuel "Emmy" Nnyanzi. No one but the Lord could have brought them together like He did back in early 2007. When they met, they both knew why and soon began a great work together. I am forever grateful to both of them, for their incredible love for their Father, and for their ability to bring others along with them during this ministry journey. Without a doubt, Kiconco and Emmy have shown me that the God we serve is SO MUCH MORE than we could ever hope or imagine. I love you both.

Many thanks also to my two children, Bailey and Libby (known in Uganda as "Mbabazi" and "Kyomu") for their ability to hear God's voice at such a young age and go serve Him willingly wherever He is calling. I am so proud to call you my daughters and know He has great plans for you both. You have been so patient with your earthly father and mother these past few years. "Webale" (thank you). You now have hundreds of brothers and sisters.

Thank you so much also to my new good friend Patrick Butler. Everybody that knows you, knows your God given gift of writing. I am grateful that you have now seen with your very own eyes what the Lord is doing on the other side of the world in Uganda. There is no better person in the world to share this amazing story of what Jesus is doing with hundreds of people on both sides of the Atlantic than you my friend. You and your wife Janet will forever be treasures to us at Parental Care Ministries (PCM).

Thank you also to Group M7 in Tyler, Texas. Your graphic design skills and high-tech talents have blessed our ministry from the very first day we met you. This book would not have made it to print or to the web without your mighty contributions.

Many blessings to all of you who have supported PCM, are supporting us, or hope to in the future. We are so thankful to partner with you and the many children and pastors of Uganda.

Continue to pray for this ministry that we may be able to show compassion to others throughout the world like Jesus commanded us in Luke 10:37: "Go and do likewise."

—*Mark "Epa" Barret MD*
Executive Director,
Parental Care Ministries

INTRODUCTION

Returning in June 2011 by jet from Uganda, I sat next to a 27-year-old Ugandan environmental engineer working in Northern Uganda. I had been investigating Parental Care Ministries (PCM) in Mbarara in a remote southwestern district.

His job was the ecological restoration of land in the north made desolate from years of attrition by rebel groups, such as the Lord's Resistance Army. My job was to verify if God was actually bringing spiritual hope, spiritual healing and practical help to orphan children in the south.

The people in the north—especially the children—he said "were in a sad state." Morale was better than years previously, he said, but still "alarmingly low." There were many orphans, he added.

I showed him a photo of Pastor Emmanuel "Emmy" and Sarah "Super-mom" Nnyanzi surrounded by a couple of dozen of the 600 orphans the pair look after at PCM, the very photo on the cover of this book.

He examined the photo carefully, then said incredulously,

"These children are orphans? They look happier than if they had parents. Why is that, please?"

That's what I had gone to Uganda to find out, after speaking with Emmy in Texas a month earlier.

As a former Religion journalist for a Texas newspaper, I had interviewed "Emmy" in the same fashion I'd spoken to many well-known—and somewhat known—people about their faith; Olympic gymnast Mary Lou Retton, pro golfer Bernhard Langer, author Philip Yancy, speaker Ruth Bell Graham the daughter of Billy Graham, film producer Ralph Winter, football great Earl Campbell, singer Toby Mac, rock musician Jim Fielder of Blood, Sweat and Tears and syndicated columnist Cal Thomas to name a few. I also have a long interview list of deeply spiritual men and women—some who lead global efforts and whose names might be recognizable, or maybe not, who represent millions of dollars and thousands of employees or volunteers doing "good works" around the globe.

I mention this because after speaking with Emmy I realized he was a genuine and rare example of a truly refined follower of God; startlingly simple and humble, genuinely loving, yet razor sharp in depth and wisdom.

Emmy possesses a remarkably uncluttered spirit seemingly unhindered by self-consciousness, fear, doubt and most importantly, bitterness, manipulation or pride. It was quite refreshing and more than a bit of a revelation to interview him.

That's why I ended up in Africa. It's one thing to "play for the press" in comfortable America. What was the man really like in Uganda?

Emmy seems to be the person most spiritual people want to become. He is humble and compassionate, yet dynamic. He seems unaware of the significance of what he has achieved, so it demands investigating. In Uganda, I was hoping to discover "the secret" of how he had discovered the peace, security, and Christ-assuredness he daily walks in. We all need to know "how he did it."

After many in-depth interviews and seeing the work of PCM in Uganda, I was convinced; Emmy would be in demand worldwide if people recognized the pearl they have in this man. His story of escape from bitterness to peace just by itself is quite remarkable—not to mention the successful ministry now following Jesus.

What I found in Africa was far beyond my expectations. It was also beyond the expectations of those members of Team 10 who went to Mbarara for the first time; and evidently those of most people who visit PCM, that I've spoken with later.

We all soon realized Emmy was not the only prize in Mbarara; it was the kids at Parental Care he and Sarah and dedicated staff loved right into the light of Christ. Team 10 was highly inspired and deeply impressed with the unforgettable sights and sounds of these orphaned children in daily action—especially the sounds of "unfiltered love" as one team member put it—as they lived their lives in front of us.

It is not a stretch of the imagination to envision these children as bearers of a spiritual future, carrying the unquenchable light of Christ into a world now slowly slipping into a confusing and debilitating spiritual darkness.

Why and how Emmy, Sarah, Mark, Monica and hundreds of PCM children and volunteers "did it" and what they did, is the context of this book. The founders, followers and fans of PCM hope the story of what they discovered inspires others to follow in God's footsteps, finding for themselves that there is so much more.

—*Patrick Butler*
Texas, USA
October 2011

Chapter One

BUILDING BLOCKS OF FLESH

"My mother is trying to kill you."

—Emmy Nnyanzi's stepsister

Young Emanuel Nnyanzi could not believe what he'd just heard. Words of dire warning continued to tumble from the lips of his sibling, but Emmy's 14-year-old mind was racing. He considered almost simultaneously his options for survival or if he should even be listening to what he was being told. Surely this could not be happening in his own home in Uganda.

He tuned into the words once again to be certain and the moving mouth once again came alive to his ears.

"I'm telling you," his stepsister was saying again. "Watch out. Don't eat tonight's food. It's been poisoned. My mother is trying to kill you. Pretend to take it, but throw it away."

Emmy could only stare silently back blankly, wondering what to do next.

As she began to leave, Emmy's stepsister said over her shoulder, "It's your decision whether to believe me or not, but whatever you do, don't eat it."

Alone with this warning, Emmy agonized at the choice before him and what it signaled. If it were true, his life at his father's house in Mbarara was over, if he survived or not. Life hadn't been good since his mother divorced his alcoholic father for marital unfaithfulness years earlier. To make matters worse, she had left the home without her son; leaving him under the control of a man who didn't really care.

A quick succession of stepmothers, 13 of them, had taken turns "caring" for the child of another woman while struggling with their own. Favoring their own children above him, Emmy slowly became aware that he didn't count.

Abuse takes many forms but parental neglect may be a particularly slow harshness, dripping out deadly doses of rejection during a period of years. It is surely one of the most biting and acidic ointments to the soul, Emmy's soul.

Emmy was surviving physically but slowly dying in spirit. He took some spiritual solace from his former years as a Catholic altar boy, but soon the form of religion had lost its appeal and ability to assuage his soul, leaving him scarred once again. He had no connections to a church or believers anywhere.

Now, this revelation; poison; attempted murder. A crime against state, soul and God's Spirit in his own household. The end of the road. The end of all pretenses at family or parental love. Not wanting to accept the raw reality of life and death, Emmy nonetheless fed the evening meal to a pig in the farm pen and waited.

In the morning the pig had died and Emmy had quietly left the house, shutting the door on his entire life which was suddenly and without anticipation, behind him. Lying to one of his father's truck drivers, he hitched a quiet and lonely ride to Kampala 125 miles, 250 kilometers away, with the excuse that he was on an errand for his father.

"I was devastated," Emmy said. "Someone had tried to kill me in my own household. I had no idea what the future would be like for me."

Finally arriving in the city and stepping out into the crowded confusion that Kampala is, Emmy slipped into the safety of anonymity, out of reach of his would-be-killer. The sorry scene was the defining moment of his young life.

For all intents and purposes, his childhood was over.

Mark

Mark Barret's mother often made brownies, perfectly cut and squared for the neighborhood children. Raised by the hands of a loving mother and wise father in the heart of America, Tennessee, he described life as idyllic as a "Leave it to Beaver" episode.

His mother, constantly playing hostess to his friends, is where young Mark learned what he called "Service 101."

He went to school and became a champion youth soccer player. He attended church with both his role-model parents who believed God was more than just a good idea located on the periphery of daily life. From his father, who was gifted in relationships, Mark learned how to love people. Harsh words were never spoken at the Barret household.

It was at a church confirmation class in 1975, the ceremony and celebration where children make the public decision to follow Jesus that life changed for him. While standing in the back listening, 9-year-old Mark became aware of a "filling" presence so strong he almost fell off the bleachers.

As the presence enveloped him from head to toe, he understood God was coming to him. He relaxed under the strong sense of love and encouragement, not fighting what was happening to him.

The "presence" didn't seem out of place for Mark. He was at a church function with his friends. His sensitive and accepting parents had prepared him for meeting his heavenly Father on the very grounds of encouragement and love he was now experiencing. Instead of being alarmed, cautious, critical or uncaring, Mark sat silently, soaking in the comforting experience of God.

It was the defining moment of Mark Barret's childhood. This was the moment he knew beyond a shadow of a doubt that God was with him.

Mark didn't share his vision of God's love and presence with his parents or anyone else. He somehow knew the experience was an unusual event, meant for him and he kept it that way. But the guiding force and light in all he would do later, eventually would come back to, and was rooted in, the experience of God's all-encompassing and all-powerful love and presence.

Monica

Monica Kennedy's parents lost a baby boy to Sudden Infant Death Syndrome before Monica was born in Austin, Texas. Her parents never fully got over the loss and despite, or perhaps because of, the counsel they received at church, they stopped attending. The painful experience created the tone and tenor of the household Monica was raised in. She never knew these facts nor fully recognized the consequences of them during her childhood.

With no spiritual anchor in the home, familial love became strangely distant and was even perceived as outright rejection, though rejection was not the spoken motivation of her parents. This was the seedbed of silenced pain where Monica lived, breathed and moved in on a daily basis. That pain was such a regular feature of life, it seemed to have always been there.

Before she was born, little Monica's life was to be defined by remorse, rejection and a sense of sorrow.

As the family slid into alternative means of comfort—alcoholism became a "stronghold" in the family—Monica felt more than ever that she was further away from parental love. Her mother kept pointing back to God despite her own struggles with depression and alcohol but her father had completely abandoned faith until much later in life.

Among her siblings, Monica felt estranged from her parents. Her young soul cried out for the love of the Father, seemingly unanswered. The parental care she needed, though she loved her parents, was absent in the home. It was the beginning of a heartbreak, a cry for healing that would reach far into her adult life.

Sarah

Sarah Nnyanzi's young life was so painful; she would rather not talk about it. Suffice it to say that she suffered a similar fate as Emmy—her mother divorced her father when Sarah was so young, she does not recall it. A series of stepmothers did nothing for the girl but keep her body alive, even accusing her character to her own father.

The defining moment of her childhood was that she was spiritually dead inside at a young age. When she was 13 years old, something happened at school that would give her a glimmer of life. This, perhaps, helped her to hang on until she could find Emmy and the pair became one—in healing, hope and ministry to hundreds of children such as themselves.

Chapter Two

CHRISTMAS CARD

It all started, as all stories do, with a dream. But before the dreams of the stories come true, there is always a problem that must be met with perseverance and faith.

Monica Barret was prepared to follow her faith the day her third-grade daughter, Libby, came home bearing a gift from Jesus. The present was wrapped up as a simple Christmas card, the result of a class project. It was a gift that would change Monica's life, and the lives of her family, forever.

"I had been feeling stuck as a Christian at times," Monica said. "I was walking around feeling rejected sometimes, sometimes dejected, you name it. It was hard to see the blessings of God in my life to tell the truth because I was dead in my thinking. I knew there was more, but what? What God started to do at that point was unraveling my thinking."

It was Christmas, 2006.

"The whole year before, the Lord was showing me that He hears the cries of the poor and needy," said Monica. "He binds up the brokenhearted—He was in the process of healing my heart, let's say."

Driving in her car near her home in Tyler, Texas, Monica's life began to change.

"This is how it started," she said. "I was sitting at a stoplight and Libby's Christmas card was on the seat next to me. I picked it up and read this:

"Glory to God in the Highest and Peace on Earth to Men.
May the Christmas song the angels sang stir in our hearts again.
Dear Mom, I feel this Christmas, we should be missionaries and help the poor.
Jesus keeps pushing me to tell you. Merry Christmas, love Libby."

"I ended up having a very unusual dream soon after that," said Monica, "of a toddler, sitting in a box. His legs were hanging outside of the box and it was pouring down rain. It was nighttime and there was a single streetlight behind him. He was really still. He was trying to survive."

God had Monica Barret's attention. It was a deceptively simple device, a note from a child, that God was using to completely change the lives of hundreds of children.

me ↓   you ↓

2006

♀ Love, hibby

"Glory to God in the highest,
And peace on earth to men"
May the Christmas song
    the angels sang,
Stir in our hearts again.

Dear mom I feel
this Christmas we
should be misionaries
and help the poor.
Jesus keeps pushing
me to tell you.
    merry Christmas!

11

Chapter Three

SO MUCH MORE

"They don't have anything, but they lack nothing."

—Dr. Foy Forehand II, PCM Team 10 member

MBARARA, Uganda, 2011—Intense, wonderfully bright sunshine struck then bounced off deep green hills behind the children and the slow-moving Rwizi river. Sunlight saturated the tops of hills in front of them in fiery orange embers as shadows slowly put the land to sleep. The total effect created a kind of canyon of comforting light that seemed to be wrapping its warm rays around the children as they prepared to worship.

It was May 2011 and Team 10 from Parental Care Ministries (PCM) was visiting.

Amazingly to the team, there was a palpable sense of God's peace in this valley "so far away" in so "unlikely a spot" as an economically poor school compound on a dirt road in rural Uganda. Except this place was neither "unlikely" to God nor the children. It was their home and the daily meeting place between them.

Some children had changed from school uniforms into their one set of fresh clothes. Djembe drums were brought out. A small group of students stood in front facing the others, starting a happy rhythm. Soon the air was full of singing, rejoicing.

The once nearly murdered Pastor Emmy stood off to the side, smiling with two hands clasped by his lips as if immensely enjoying the scene.

Suddenly, through crescendo and diminuendo as the children danced, worshipped and celebrated, an astonishing otherworldly sense of encouragement seemed to spring from the sound. And more than encouragement; a startling sense of revelation, of closeness and intimacy with God, an awareness of His presence—not merely the belief that God was present, but an awareness that He actually was.

Three visiting adults and five teenagers from Texas seemed almost stunned into silence by the intimacy of what they were hearing and seeing. The teenagers unreservedly showed broad smiles as they sat against the wall of the school courtyard, soaking in the scene; what was happening was too beautiful to grasp intellectually.

"You can't comprehend this with the mind," said Tyler Forehand, 16, a musician. "But you can really understand it with the heart."

"Wow," gushed Hannah Gill, 16, as she picked up a smiling little girl, cuddling her in her arms. "This is incredible. It's like God is here."

God really seemed to be among the orphaned children, freely lavishing his love upon them simply because they expected Him to be there with them. And these "poor" children, rich in awareness of God's presence, seemed to know what to do, how to respond, act and behave with their heavenly Father, completely comfortable with the presence of an eternal, loving Spirit.

It was also a completely compelling scene, much harder avoiding than witnessing.

"The thing about this," said Mark Barret, laughing a little without taking his eyes off the children as they worshipped, "is that these kids don't know what they're doing is special. They think we worship like this in America."

The children appeared delightfully unaware what they were experiencing was unique or that they were engaging a tone and tenor almost unknown in American churches. They did not know they had entered into what many Christians in the West have sought and been largely unable to achieve to this degree; deep intimacy with God.

To these children, being bathed in the love, joy and comfort of God was normal, everyday Christianity. They reveled in the relationship they were enjoying between themselves and their all-loving Father God. No expression seemed too intimate to hold back as they raised hands, arms and voices to the air.

Mark laughed again, shaking his head and raising his eyebrows, as he listened.

"It's incredible," he said. "Look at these children. Do they seem sad? See how small that one is over there," he said, pointing to a little girl. "Her name is Milly."

Milly had changed from her school uniform to her one, purple flowered dress. She knelt with her forehead to the hard ground, deep in prayer.

Soon all the students, some appearing as young as 5 years old would stop singing and begin to pray and praise as a group, words tumbling out in rapid-fire expression. Some stood in prayer, faces lifted to the sky. Some were kneeling on the ground. Other children as small as Milly, girls and boys, knelt beside her with hands in the air or covering their faces as they prayed aloud, sounding like a babbling brook of continuous praise.

With hundreds of hands lifted high, engrossed in prayer and speaking thankfully to the presence of an omnipresent Spirit, it was hard to imagine God would not send these very children from Uganda to bring the blessing of intimacy to the world, helping people to praise.

"There are grown men and women in America who have been Christians all their lives who can't do this," Mark said in a confidential tone and in wonderment. "I learn something from these children every time I come here. It's as if, you know, this is real church."

The team would later discuss how easy it was to imagine and wonder, "Were these the future examples of believers who would declare to Christians and others alike, even in America, that there was so much more of a loving God; so accepting and willing to impart life to all who would come to Him?"

It was somewhat intoxicating to even imagine that sweet scenario while watching the precious children sing.

Team 10 member Rocky Gill said, "When I see these children and realize how little they own in the world, then see how they worship God, it makes me think 'We have ruined our children in America.' We certainly have something to learn from them. They have so much more than we do."

Waiting his turn during the singing to speak a few words of encouragement to the children, Dr. Foy Forehand II of the Texas team displayed a bit of perplexity and admiring amazement as he wondered aloud how he would "follow" such a move of intimacy with Christ. The praise and "presence" seemed never-ending as they continued to sing.

"These children don't have anything," he said quietly, looking down at his glasses in his hand as he cleaned them. Putting his glasses back on he looked up and surveyed the still-singing children, folding his arms tightly across his chest.

"They don't have anything" he said, nodding approvingly, looking around and smiling, "but they lack nothing."

It was a comprehensive conclusion by the doctor, succinctly summing up the surpassing spiritual presence of a remarkable place called Parental Care Ministries, Mbarara, Uganda.

Web Extra: See and hear the children at PCM Mabarara worship captured on video at http://www.youtube.com/watch?v=YyVD1jlH4uU

Chapter Four

PARENTAL CARE MINISTRIES

"It was like nothing I've ever heard before.
The sound will stay with me the rest of my life."

—Rocky Gill

Right now, today, there are nearly a thousand orphan and needy children at Parental Care Ministries. They are in the care of Emmy and Sarah Nnyanzi and their dedicated staff of teachers and workers at five school locations.

A sixth location, the largest of them all, is being built on 68 acres of pristine and prime land at a place called Katyazo (Cat-Yah-Zo). The new school is 19 miles from where the worship had taken place in Mbarara, currently the largest school with more than 300 boarder students. The PCM School in remote, mountainside Rwemikoma has about 200 children attending classes, but no live-in students. The PCM School in nearby Ibanda has four classrooms and two small "sleeping rooms" where some of the 100 students live. Two schools in Kyasenya and Minekye have been started.

All these children have in the world is what they can fit in the size of small trunk—a box is more accurate—at the foot of their bunk beds.

The addition of beds for students to sleep in was a thankful step up, really. Until recently all the children slept on thin foam mats, some with ragged torn edges. The worn foam now sits in the corners of the large, concrete, dormitory-like rooms built by volunteers working with Nigel and Marian Whitaker and PCM UK in Wales.

The foam mats remain for the children not yet having beds.

It was through the efforts of Parental Care Ministries USA that beds began to arrive, along with a clean water well, school uniforms, textbooks, food and medicine.

In May of 2011, the eight members of Team 10 did two things no other PCM Texas group had done since the first trip by the Barret family in 2008: They visited Queen Elizabeth National Park at the Mountains of the Moon, traveling extensively through the countryside, seeing for themselves "up-close" how the rural people look and live.

Secondly, and most significantly it turned out, they spent a night in the semi-open air dormitories with the PCM children at Mbarara.

They also took a rare visit to the mountainside PCM school at ruggedly splendorous Rwemikoma, accessible only by dirt roads which are nearly non-existent when it rains. Only a handful of PCM teams have gotten to go to enchanting and remote Rwemikoma.

Each groundbreaking and adventurous act brought its own unique blessings for Team 10. At Rwemikoma they delivered the first-ever school lunches, the first of a year's supply, to the happy and grateful students. The lunches were provided by a single Sunday School class in America, touched by the costly drilling of a disappointing dry water well months earlier.

On the road to Queen Elizabeth park, Team 10 got a bird's eye overview of the lush, hilly, banana and tea plantations of Uganda, called the "Pearl of Africa" by Winston Churchill. They saw how village after village was filled with busy, adequately dressed and fed men, women and children going about their daily business, carrying themselves with a sense of controlled purpose, peace and even pleasure.

The desperate poverty of India or the despair of Haiti was not visible. There is hope for the infrastructure of Uganda.

But the crown, the pinnacle of new experiences for Team 10 was the "sleepover" in Mbarara. Traveling each day a short distance from a comfortable hotel to the school, it was the five teenagers of the group instigating the overnighter. Somehow their enthusiasm captured the imaginations of the adults who, at the last minute, decided not to be outdone by their youngsters and joined them.

It proved to be one of the most ascending experiences of their lives as children happily shared what little they had with their "American friends." What the team especially noticed was how the children woke up in the morning.

"I was lying in my bunk in the dorms," said Rocky Gill, "when the boys started to wake up. While still in his bed, one boy, Jude, began to sing praise to God. He was joined by another, and soon the entire room seemed to be singing."

The song Jude sang was "Thank You, Jesus." As the sounds of early morning devotion enveloped the room with an other worldly sense of purpose and hope, Rocky, Tyler, Foy and Mark caught each other's eyes, smiling at what they were hearing.

"It was like nothing I've ever heard before," Rocky said. "The sound will stay with me the rest of my life."

Web Extra: *See and hear "Thank You, Jesus" by Jude himself set to a PCM slideshow at http://www.youtube.com/watch?v=pU7Nq5Myrv8*

Chapter Five

MISERY IN MOZAMBIQUE

"OK, God, you've got my attention.
What do you want me to do?"

—Monica Barret

Monica Barret found herself at a ministry in Mozambique deeply in doubt, shortly after her daughter Libby had given her the Christians card. It was January 2007 as she sought God for answers while living in a little hut with three other ladies. God did not seem to be present.

Feeling out of place with nowhere to go, she prayed, "God, what in the world am I doing here in Africa?" With her face in the pillow, she sighed.

"You know I'm not a traveler, Lord. You know I want to do Your will. I thought You were drawing me here, but now I feel so out of place."

She turned over on her back and stared towards the thatched roof she could not see. There was no answer from God. It had been a couple of days since she had ventured from the room, her nagging discomfort preventing her from participating.

It was just six weeks after she'd received the Christmas card that had changed her mind and life direction. She looked up into the darkness trying to recall the steps that had taken her 10,000 miles from home, by herself, without her husband, far from her family. Confirmation that she had heard and done the right thing seemed to come from everywhere.

"After I had read Libby's card," she said later, "I had gone home, knelt on the kitchen floor and said, 'OK, God, you've got my attention. What do you want me to do?'"

She waited until clarity came.

"I remembered I was reading a book about an orphanage ministry in Mozambique," she said. "Then the name of someone I knew also came to mind. God said, "Call." I did and guess what? They were planning a trip to Mozambique to the very ministry I had been reading about."

After talking about the upcoming trip to Mozambique, Monica was invited to go along. Afterwards, she was certain God had directed her path. Mozambique she was sure, was the next step.

And Africa was a huge step for her.

There had been little security in the home Monica Kennedy had grown up in. Sometimes the insecure memories of her upbringing were still with her, even as an adult, even as a believer in Christ. Despite all the teaching and faithfully attending church, it was as if childhood memories were somehow embedded in her very cellular being.

"My parents tried to drown their sorrows in alcohol and it became a "stronghold," a serious life-controlling problem in their lives," she said. "There was dissension in our extended family, too. I never could understand where that came from."

Faith flickered like a weak candle in the household of her youth, but was not completely blown out.

"Mom believed in Christ and read the Bible daily, but Dad didn't come to Christ until he was 40," she said. "He never had a background in the Word (the Bible); because of that there was verbal abuse, chaos, you name it. There was hardly any stability at home. We didn't go to church, but I had friends who did. If they asked me to go then I went."

One night an especially significant event took place.

"A friend asked me to a Billy Graham crusade," she said. "That's where I officially gave my life to Christ. I was 12 years old."

"One other thing about home," Monica said. "Dad was an orphan while he was growing up."

Monica met Mark while in college in Texas. He was tall, athletic and studious. "Everyone called Mark "Bub" in college, so I would say "Hi, Bub," to him now and then," she said.

Mark liked Monica, but thought she was "too cool" for a guy like him.

"I never talked to her because I figured she just had to be dating someone," he said. "When I found out she wasn't, I couldn't believe it. I went for it."

Waiting until life provides an opening and then fully pursuing it has always been part of his character.

"I'd never been the dating type," he said. "My thinking has always been, 'find the right thing to do and when you find it, go all in.' When you become a Christian, really do it. Go all in. If you're going to get married, then do it. For life."

Mark and Monica soon married for life in June of 1990. Mark studied pediatrics and then started a medical practice. Times were lean, he said, until he got started.

"We didn't see many nickels until I was 29," he said. "Then everything good started happening."

The happy couple had two children, Bailey then Libby. Living in Tyler, Texas, life was good. The Barrets moved into a large house in a gated section of an exclusive neighborhood. They became part of a social network that appreciated what a physician had to say. That social platform would cause some troubling side effects and new doors would open later. But for now, all seemed well.

Except all was not completely well with Monica's soul. She knew it, deep down, no matter what appearances communicated otherwise. By the time Libby was in third grade and Bailey was 11 years old, life was building to a conflict in her heart.

"I felt stuck as a Christian and I didn't know why," she said. "I couldn't act upon what I felt in my heart for Jesus. Honestly, I was sort of fed up."

One day Monica wandered through her neatly organized, tastefully and well-decorated spacious rooms. The kitchen, dining room and sitting areas were colorfully organized and situated perfectly for conversation, reading or inspiration. Sunlight flooded the rooms for peaceful, easy-on-the-eyes viewing. She gazed outside where workers kept her perfectly manicured yard. Varieties of colorful, interesting birds fed at the ornate feeders outside the window.

Soul-soothing sitting areas in the front, side and back of the two-story white hardy board plantation home, invited her to relax, enjoy the "good life" and reflect on the scriptures that said the home of the wise would be filled with "good treasures." What more could she want?

There was something wrong with the pretty picture though, even as Monica was confessing that Christ was her King, thanking Him continuously for all she had.

She walked through her home, carefully considering her thoughts. As she entered her bedroom, she suddenly yelled, "Jesus I love you!" at the top of her lungs.

"What happened when I shouted 'Jesus,'" she said, "was that it seemed as if I could actually see the words of Galatians 2:20 hanging in the air. '...and I no longer live, but Christ lives in me. The life I live in the flesh, I live by faith in the Son of God, who loved me and gave Himself up for me.'"

Clarity came again.

"It was as if God were showing me a key," she said. "I could suddenly see I was letting my flesh walk instead of walking by the Spirit. The reality is, I'm a new person and I wasn't letting that new person live. Even though I had blessing after blessing with my husband, my daughters, my house, I couldn't really see them to tell the truth, because I was so dead in my thinking."

All of that was about to change, not only for Monica but also for the entire Barret household. What would come soon was more than any of them could think or imagine.

Chapter Six

MESSAGE IN A MAGAZINE

"May the Christmas song the angels sang
stir in our hearts again."

—Libby Barret

After Libby's Christmas card prodded her to seek God's direction in her "stuck" Christian life, it was time to advise her best friend, Mark, of her thoughts and see what he would say.

Going to her husband with what she had, Monica would find Mark was less than thrilled.

"Honey, honestly, c'mon and be reasonable," said the practical, university-educated rationalist. "It's hard for you to get to Dallas and back. That's only 90 miles away. You want me to say I'm OK with you going to Africa?"

"I'll be with a group," Monica said. "It's not like I'm going by myself."

Mark, the physician, responded quickly.

"There is a lot of serious disease out there, you know; yellow fever, tuberculosis, malaria—and God only knows what crazy rebel groups may be running around with guns."

"If God is saying 'go,' I'll be safe," she said.

Mark shook his head. The needy husband emerged.

"No, I need you here. It's winter and that's the time I see most of my patients," he said. "It will be too hard on me if you're not here. Who will take care of Libby and Bailey—and me? I don't think so. "

The door had seemed to be slammed shut—hard—but Monica began to pray.

"I just knew Libby's card had been God speaking to us through our children," she said. "I knew I was supposed to go to Mozambique even if Mark didn't, but God had to be the one to show him. I wasn't going to be able to do it."

God began to work on Mark Barret. As Monica prayed, Mark began to review his reactions to his wife's inclinations. To his way of thinking, Monica's ideas were all out of order.

"The first thing wrong was that Libby's card was not addressed to me," Mark said as he recalled reasoning it through. "The card said, 'Dear Mom' not 'Dear Mom and Dad.'

"The other thing was that God was not talking to me about it. Why? Why would God talk to my wife about Africa and not me?"

Mark even slightly mocked Monica's idea to a close confidant—and was surprised by the response.

"Our best friends from Michigan came over that very night," Mark said, "and I showed them Libby's card."

"Look at this card Monica gave me today," Mark had laughed, handing the homemade Christmas reminder to his friend, Daniel. "My wife wants to go to Africa in the middle of winter instead of taking care of me when we're seeing so many patients. That's not going to happen."

Daniel Wallace had worked in ministry for years. His wisdom and understanding was a bulwark to Mark's own spiritual perspective. Mark respected his friend's faith walk and wise words. He waited to be supported in his decision to quash Monica's Africa "adventure."

Instead of laughing along, Daniel had slowly surveyed Libby's Christmas card that read, "Glory to God in the Highest." A hand-drawn picture of an angel, God's ministering entities and the heart view of a child's faith, was prominently displayed on the front.

Daniel had been in ministry too long to easily brush aside promptings of God through children. His eye fell on Libby's hand-drawn words, "May the Christmas song the angels sang stir in our hearts again."

The words struck a spiritual chord in Daniel's own heart as he knew how many times he'd encouraged others to let God stir their hearts, and how often he'd needed it himself. He did not want his friends to miss what God may have in store for them. He pursed his lips, and nodded.

"Well," Daniel simply said, handing the card back to Mark, "Did you pray about it?" and looked at his friend with an honest, questioning gaze.

Mark was stunned by his friend's simple response. As he listened, he realized he was being told something he needed to learn; ask God even when the most unlikely or uncomfortable scenarios might come your way; ask for wisdom; ask for direction; ask for the highest good, not the "best for me." Ask and, "I will answer you. I will counsel you with my eye upon you."

Mark shook his head at the memory of Daniel's surprise question.

"The thing is, they are never at our home because they live so far away," said Mark. "At the very moment I needed some wise input, there it was. I couldn't just ignore what he said, and I couldn't ignore God either."

Though later, Mark gave "ignoring God" a try anyway.

Faced with the "new next step" his friend had pointed out, Mark began the next leg of his faith journey on rocky road. God must have patiently sighed when he heard His son pour out his complaint—and demand.

"Look Lord," Mark prayed that night, "You've got to tell me, too. I'm not sending my wife out on an unknown trip with unknown group for an unknown purpose."

In days to come the couple prayed and talked about what God was doing in their lives, but as the Christmas season was about to descend upon them, no decision was made about Africa. Time was running out for plane tickets, shots and arrangements. Either it was Africa or not. Which? Choose.

Mark went back to God at the end of the last day before a Christmas break.

"OK, God, Tell me. Speak to me," Mark said with a combination of expectancy and wonderment. "Tell me what you want her to do."

The response to Mark's request was odd, he recalled.

"I thought God said, 'Go get the mail.' That was kind of strange," Mark said.

Mark paused while he tried to consider rationally what he was receiving as an answer to prayer.

"Yeah, OK, I'll go get the mail," Mark finally said semi-sarcastically and out loud to no one in particular. "What harm can that do?" he thought. "People get the mail every day."

But there was only one important item in the mailbox this time—a Christian magazine. Mark went back to the office and regarded it. Nothing special, he thought. The cover story was about ministry in a red light district in Thailand.

"Hmmppf," thought Mark, "not the kind of holiday reading I was wanting to read to my kids."

He tossed the magazine aside, but there was an immediate reaction.

"It was crazy," Mark said, "but I thought God said, 'No, no. Open it up. Look through it,' so I did, not really believing any of this was from God."

But in the back of the magazine was a story he suddenly knew he could not avoid. The hairs on his neck began to tingle.

"The article was by a woman," said Mark, "who went to Africa. By herself. To the exact tiny village Monica wanted to go to. The title of the article was "Surprised by Friendship: Discovering Where Hope Begins in a Village—in Mozambique."

Wide-eyed, he began reading. His entire being was soon electrified by a scant section buried deep in the story. It was as if bells were going off in his head as he inhaled the words he was reading.

"My journey did not begin with a life long desire to be a missionary in Africa," Mark read. "The desire came when I began realizing there is more to life then pursuing personal comfort with which I had surrounded myself; a graduate degree, a nice car, a safe job...I hoped Africa would save me from a life of numbness, a life of mere satisfaction, seeking more; more money, more recognition, more whatever. I hoped to find it true that 'less was more.'"*

Stunned and surprised by the sequence of events, Mark knew beyond a doubt that God was speaking to him about his lifestyle, his direction and his ultimate purpose. Alone with the silence in his doctor's office he had worked so hard to establish, he held the magazine in his hands—the tool God was using to draw him into an unexplainable reality that would be so much more than he could possibly think or imagine; a remarkable spiritual reality that would bless him and his family beyond their ability to ask.

"No," Mark said out loud, firmly. "No! She's not going."

He threw the magazine on the floor and went home.

---

*Zinchini, Cassandra. "Surprised by Friendship," (Christianity Today online, 11, January, 2007)

Chapter Seven

BATTLING BITTERNESS

"It was worse than what I had left—except
they didn't try to kill me."

—Emmy Nnyanzi

"Nnyanzi, come here you worthless village fool," shrieked a tyrannical, matronly voice. As Emmy the houseboy, 15, arrived in the room of his new employers in Kampala—a wealthy family—the mother of the house grabbed his ears and painfully pulled on them, dragging him across the room. Her children, about his age, were present and laughing at Emmy's pain and humiliation.

"How many times have I told you to turn off the TV when we leave, simple one?" she said loudly, pointing to the television. "Have you not learned what an 'off' switch is yet, villager?" She began to hit Emmy in the head as he raised his arms to protect himself. He could hear her children laughing through his upraised arms around his ears, even through the sounds of her slapping. His feelings burned with broken self-worth, anger. He was completely humiliated.

"And stop begging my children to teach you how to use these things, Nnyanzi" she said, still beating him. "You are their servant; they are not yours. I brought you here to work for my children, not for them to work for you. Learn it for yourself or leave."

Turning to her children, she said, "This is why you are better than simple villagers who don't even know what electricity is or how to turn off lights," she said. "Don't forget. You are not like them."

Pushing Emmy backwards, she said, "Go away, useless child. Clean the house. You can do that at least, I think."

When Emmy had run away from home after the poisoned pig died at his father's house, the slender and small boy had found work as a domestic servant, a houseboy, for a prominent family in Kampala. The situation was better than death, he said, but not by much.

"They treated me badly, worse than my many stepmothers at home," said Emmy. "They were abusive. The mother particularly worked me like a slave, continuously belittling me in front of her own children. There was no love, no acceptance, not even courtesy. It was worse than what I had left, except they didn't try to kill me."

Suffering now from the rejection of his mother who had abandoned him to his alcoholic, inattentive father and uncaring multiple spouses, to enduring the life of an abused servant-slave, Emmy decided to leap once again; and again seemed to run aground on rocks.

His solution to the soul-killing "houseboy" situation was a day laborer's job, which soon put him in physical peril. Emmy was 16. Working to the bone at apartment building construction sites, he cleared rubble and heavy rock with a wheelbarrow, hour after hour, day after day, for weeks and months.

"It was such hard work, I soon began to bleed internally," Emmy said. "We worked from sunup to sundown. I was often sick and weak. I could not eat after a while."

"You have to be a man to work here, Nnyanzi, " the work boss chided him one day. "You said you could do this job but you don't look like you can take it. We can't make it easy for you just because you're like a child. Why don't you quit before you fall down?"

Emmy knew he couldn't quit. It was either death by starvation or by exhaustion. He would not become a criminal and steal as he knew others did.

Faced with only those choices, he looked again for a way to run, a way out. He just didn't know what, where or how it could possibly happen. Even though he knew God was there, he almost never prayed.

Almost miraculously, though, a man who owned a primary school somehow saw a spark in the worked-to-the-bone teenager. It was a glimmer of promise that Emmy could be good for another type of work.

"You're smart. You'd be a good school teacher," Geofrey Kiyaaga had told Emmy one day. "If you come for training and apply yourself, I'll give you a job in my school."

Young Emmy jumped at the chance and took the training. Studying hard, learning how to do lesson plans, at just age 17 he became a trained educator for Kiyaaga, teaching the P3 and P5 (elementary school) levels.

"I believe I would have died if he had not come to offer me a way out," Emmy said. "I was saved from death."

Emmy loved what he was doing, encouraging children. In their tender, young faces he often saw the same looks he'd once had at their age. His heart went out to them, daily.

Emmy also found another consolation and love about a year later. He met Sarah and as they talked about their lives, the two realized they had much in common. Sarah had "met Jesus" years earlier when Bible teachers from Scripture Union had come to her school. She was 13 years old when she "gave her life" to Christ, but she didn't take it very seriously. She also came from a divorced home and stepmothers who neglected her, accusing her falsely to her father.

They were married in 1989. He was 19 years old. Sarah was 18.

They were happy together and relatively stable. They were living very modestly, but it didn't matter. They had each other. But there was so much more God wanted to bless them with if only the happy pair would look to Him.

As they were preparing to move into town closer to the school, God suddenly intervened. Emmy's attention and direction were arrested when he heard a voice, amplified by loud speakers.

The streets were crowded. As people ran towards the blaring sound and packed themselves around a platform, Emmy wondered what in the world was going on. It was preacher Joseph Sserwadda holding a crusade in Nakivubo. Moving up through the crowd, edging his way to the front so he could see, he was soon being touched by God.

"Jesus says 'Come to me all you who are weary and burdened and I will give you rest,'" Sserwadda said. "The Bible says, 'Take my yoke upon you and learn from me; for I am gentle and humble in heart and you will find rest for your souls, for my yoke is easy and my burden is light.' Jesus knows what you've been through, where you're coming from. He knows where you are. He knows where He wants to take you; to a blessing. Why don't you come to Him, now?"

It was a good question, Emmy thought. Why didn't he give his life to God? As a former altar boy, Emmy had heard about Jesus but he didn't know Him. Not like Pastor Sserwadda was saying. Still, he wasn't sure.

Looking past the heads in the crowd towards the front, the preacher was saying there was so much more to life. The loudspeaker sound seemed to diminish and Emmy's thoughts turned towards the future.

He had to think about Sarah who he had just recently married, and their future family. He remembered the faces of the children he taught every day. He knew what some of them were going through, just as he and Sarah had. How would they be saved from a fate like theirs, he wondered?

Feeling alone in the crowded street, his heart was touched as he realized God was with him and had been all along. He'd seen everything Emmy had been through. Emmy looked up at the sky, down to his shoes, back to the speaker in front of him. He knew in his heart it was time. He knew what he had to do now.

A moment later, Emmy Nnyanzi finally stopped running and gave his life completely to Jesus.

"Yes, I would have died if Geofrey Kiyaaga had not seen a spark in me worth developing," said Emmy, "but I would have died spiritually if I did not come to Jesus. Jesus sees in us something worth developing, even more than a man."

Having met Jesus already, Sarah now followed in Emmy's spiritual footsteps. The couple realized there was more God wanted to give them than they were able to find. Life.

Even while being grateful for their new lives, what Emmy and Sarah could not forget, what they chose not to remand to the recesses of their memories, was the parental love they had missed for so many years. Soon would come a realization that would change their lives and the lives of hundreds of others, forever.

Chapter Eight

NEAR SPIRITUAL DESTRUCTION

"A child will live with almost nothing if they are truly loved. But if they are not loved, you can give them everything in the world and they will not be happy."

—Emmy Nnyanzi

Sitting in a Bible study, Emmy had a revelation that had taken all of his 20 years to come to; he was still sitting near spiritual destruction, even as a relatively new Christian. And he was helping it happen.

When he was a 17-year-old educator teaching school at the P3 and P5 elementary levels, Emmy had done well. At 19 he had found love when he met Sarah.

Committing their lives to each other, they took another step and recommitted themselves to their Christian roots. Soon after giving their lives to Christ, God directed Emmy and Sarah back to the village he had come from to start a church. Starting out small, eight jobless women were the only congregants of the new tiny church.

But the small steps were slowly leading them to a conclusion they could not dream of.

First, though, there was some "underbrush," some old business to deal with.

While attending Bible lessons and studying the life of Joseph, Emmy suddenly realized how dangerously close he was to a type of spiritual death; bitterness.

"Be like Joseph and do not hold on to what has happened to you," the study leader was saying. "If you keep bitterness, it will lead you to destruction. There is nothing good in keeping bitterness."

"I have yet to forgive!" Emmy thought like a lightning flash. "I'm still hurt and angry at what happened to me."

His mouth nearly fell open at the thought of having real forgiveness towards those who had done him harm. The idea seemed all at once outrageous, hurtful, freeing, impossible - and right. Stunned and satisfied at the same time that it was God revealing this truth to him, Emmy yet resisted when he thought of the application.

"My mother left me to an unkind man," he prayed to God. "When I was 14 years old my stepmother tried to kill me, and in my own house. I did not want to believe such a thing. I have been abused and treated as a slave by a cruel, domineering woman. I have been used by manipulative men who almost worked me to death. You are asking me to forgive them?"

Sitting in the room in the Bible class, the story of Joseph's trials came back to him. Joseph's brothers tried to kill him, and sold him into slavery instead. Joseph was falsely accused and imprisoned. He was neglected and forgotten even while he did good in prison.

"What good will keeping your bitterness do you?" the leader was saying.

Going home, Emmy talked out his thoughts with Sarah concerning all they had gone through. They were still going through it to some extent, still "eating" some of the fruits of frustration and unforgiving.

"If I believe God is my loving Father, then there is purpose to all the trials I go through," Emmy said to Sarah, "but I don't know if I can forgive. I don't know if I want to forgive."

"After he forgave, Joseph saved his brothers," Sarah said. "How could he have done this without forgiving them first?"

In their own small home, Emmy and Sarah pondered what they were hearing in the Spirit, listening to what God was saying to Emmy through the life of Joseph so long ago. Emmy loved Sarah and his children. He loved teaching children new things. But he began to realize there were old things that had not yet "passed away;" the past bitterness keeping his students, and even himself, down. He could see that Joseph's brothers were ashamed after knowing he was the one who saved them.

"Joseph knew that in spite of all sorts of problems he passed through, there was a purpose in his life," Emmy said, still deep in thought. "He realized God had intended them so he could save his family. So I think now, 'all the things I have passed through, God can use them for me to be someone who can save and help others.' I have to forgive those people who hurt me from the bottom of my heart."

Sarah knew she had people to forgive, too. Emmy could not do this alone. Holding hands in their small house, they prayed, committing their path to God.

"Lord, we are new Christians," they prayed. "We don't fully know what to do.

But what we see is that Joseph never let what happened to him get in the way of his relationship with You. How can we teach children to forgive those who hurt them, and to trust You if we cannot do it? If you are our loving Father, then we believe there is purpose in everything we have passed through. We forgive everyone who hurt us, Lord. They did not know what they were doing, as you said, on the cross."

Praying with Sarah, forgiving and asking for forgiveness for the first time, was one type of challenge Emmy said, but there were deeper things to do as he worked out forgiveness in his life.

"I started looking at these people who did harm to me," Emmy said, "and thought, 'why I should become annoyed about them, bitter about them because they caused me to suffer all these things? I know God has a better plan for me. Let me do what God wants me to do.'"

He knew, at some point, he would see some of those who hurt him. He had to determine now what to do when he saw them.

Emmy decided, "Before I meet them again, I say now that I will never speak anything to them reminding them of what they did to me. But what I am going to do, I am going to do actions which will show them I am a changed person and I love them."

Emmy and Sarah had finally broken the threshold of understanding, seeing God's loving purpose as they put all the concepts of forgiveness, love and healing together.

The new perspective slowly had its effect on the couple as they began to reach out to children whose pasts were similar to their own. As their own family grew, Emmy and Sarah could not ignore the plight of other children, orphan children, who had no one to look after them.

As a pastor, Emmy did not have much money. They lived, as many of their fellow Ugandans did, in a small mud hut. It was in this setting where Emmy and Sarah first became convinced God was calling them into full-time ministry to orphan children.

By 1999, they had brought four other children in the home to live with their own four. Recalling how "houseboy" Emmy had been "separated" from the children better off than he, Emmy insisted no such distinction be made between the children in his house.

"These are your brothers and sisters," he told his children. "This is their home now, too. Love them as your family."

It was a financial stretch to reach out. Now there were eight children sleeping in a single rented room.

"A Christian friend, a woman from England saw all these children in one room and was touched," Emmy said. "She went home and raised money so we could buy a house."

It was 2002 and now the eight children had more space in a bought house. But not for long.

"Look at all this room we have," Sarah said one day. "We have too much space for ourselves. Emmy nodded his head as he looked around and smiled.

"I was thinking the same," he said. The pair knew what they were going to do. Slowly they began to add a child, here and there, to the family.

Some of the children they stumbled on as they went about their day. Friends brought by kids who were in a fix and needed help. Soon, orphans, some who had been sleeping outside or on dirt, were under the protection of the Nnyanzi rooftop; 36 kids in all, making the total number of children in the house 41.

Yes, most of them were sleeping on the floor of the house; five of them stuck their little legs comfortably under Sarah and Emmy's bed each night, giggling as they went to sleep, but even that was a definite step up from the dirt floors of mud huts. Plus, there was love; real parental care and concern, love and acceptance from Sarah and Emmy who opened their hearts to be a channel of Christ to his children. There was joy as they all shared what they had.

"A child will live with almost nothing if they are truly loved," said Emmy, "and they will be fine. But if they are not loved, you can give them everything in the world and they will not be happy."

Their family of 41 was astonishingly happy and there was contentment. But a cloud was coming on the horizon. A hard choice would have to be made soon. The bar in trusting God would be raised to a point many might simply turn back from and say, "enough."

With 41 kids in the house, Emmy and Sarah realized they had pushed past the point where they could adequately provide education for their charges. Most education in Uganda is paid for by the families of children. There was simply not enough money to go around in the Nnyanzi household.

"Let's start our own school," Emmy said to Sarah one day. Then we could teach them ourselves, and other children who would come to the school."

Sarah looked at her husband, realizing that 41 children was not enough for Emmy. There were going to be more. And if a school was going to be started, a lot more.

"Fine," Sarah said. "Where is the money going to come from to have school grounds and a building? We can't have a school here. There is no room."

Emmy considered the options.

"Well, we have a van. And a house," he said slowly. "We could…

"What, sell them?" Sarah said, wide-eyed. "Where would we live? How would we go anywhere?"

Emmy said. "Look at what God has done so far. We started out small, with four orphans, but now there are 36. Surely God can take care of more than 36 orphans He loves if we let Him."

Sarah saw in her mind's eye hundreds upon hundreds of children who needed help, all loved dearly by God. She could not resist what her husband was saying.

"But how," she asked. "How is this going to happen? We were given money to buy a house, yes, but we don't know anybody who can build us a school."

"See, God has taken us from somewhere," said Emmy. "Now we are here today and he is taking us somewhere tomorrow. It is time to grow. And we will if we trust God."

Soon the van and the house were on the market as Emmy and Sarah searched for a suitable spot to start a school. Four acres were available a few miles from Mbarara right near the banks of the Rwizi River, downstream from the city.

If they sold the house, there would be enough to rent a small house and put a down payment on the Mbarara property, but nothing left to build with. As they prayed, peace came to them that this was the direction of God. The house was sold, the van went next, the dye was cast and the next chapter in their faith journey was started.

Chapter Nine

HIRELINGS

"As for me, I believe in a big God who does big things, but He starts with small things and makes them big."

—Emmy Nnyanzi

As their ministry to children had been growing—first in the mud hut, then the house—Emmy was convinced this was God's path for him. But there was little money in the church and few "tithing contributors" to provide finances. Undeterred, Emmy and Sarah started their church anyway, with eight jobless women who made up the entire church-going congregation. He was the only man.

The tiny church could not pay for his house rent. He struggled to get food. He labored with the small group ministering and praying for them.

"What are we to do, Pastor, with such a small group like us?" One of the women said during a mud-hut meeting. "What do we have that we can use?"

Looking at his small church Emmy realized God was still working in the situation around him, teaching them all. Seeing what they "didn't have" was the wrong perspective.

"If we think we can do things on our own strength, our own vocation, our own wisdom, we will never be happy," he told them. "But when I read in Jeremiah 9:23, the Bible tells me to never boast because you are wise, because of your strength or because of your riches. But whoever should boast, should boast of one thing; that he has known Me and understood that I am the God who exercises righteousness and kindness, because I have pleasure in those."

Looking around at the faces of the faithful women, he said, "That means the one thing that would cause us to boast or be happy is that we have known God. I know that I live by His mercy, not because I am so powerful. I live by His help, not because I have a lot of money. He is the one who helped me to live, to keep on going, to do my day-to-day work. That will help us when things are worse, because we will just take refuge in Him. That is why the Bible calls God, "A strong tower." You can reach out to people just like yourselves, people who are in the same situation you are."

Emmy knew "successful" pastors in town. He was surprised how much the money was a point of ministry with them.

"In one church I knew," he said, "the pastor had plenty; a car, a house, a large stipend. But at one point, he married. He wanted more and received it. But it still wasn't enough. He demanded more salary.

Church members came to him and said, "Look here, pastor, as a single man we rented you a two-room house. But now, since you are married, we have given you a larger house for your family, self-contained, a big house. On top of that, we have raised your weekly allowance. So where do you expect us to come up with more money for you?"

"To make matters worse," said Emmy, "only two people were paying for all the extra needs of the pastor. This pastor came to me and said, 'These people are joking. I told them to give me this and this and this, but it is as if they don't care. If they don't raise it, I'm going to go.'"

"I thought he was kidding," said Emmy. "But to my surprise, he left the church."

He shook his head at the memory.

"That was amazing for me, back then, to see people with such hearts whereby if they are not paid they will leave. I could not figure out why a pastor would leave his church, abandoning people because they have not paid him what he needed. But I saw it with my own eyes. It was surprising.

"I remembered the scripture where Jesus talked about the shepherd of wages, when the wolves would attack the sheep he would run because he was only a hireling."

The "hireling" pastor story made Emmy dig in deeper to God.

"The benefits this pastor was getting from his church, I could not get them in my church," said Emmy. "But I was not willing to leave my people. I kept on, and that's when God started providing our needs. Sometimes we see those types of pastors, some who are there for the flock and those who are there for wages. God gives you a heart for your people. You love them, care for them. You are accountable for them."

Today, Emmy oversees more than 40 small churches and pastors. These pastors are passing through what Emmy had at the beginning of his own ministry. He tells his pastors to accept the small things first and trust God for growth.

"In Uganda there are many people with a 'big' vision," said Emmy. "But for years they have done nothing because all along they want to start big. They always say, 'for me, my vision is big. I don't believe in small things, because my God is big.' That's how they talk. They have come to think that vision is a matter of writing things down on paper.

"We have preachers here in Uganda, when you are inviting them, they want a big congregation; and the congregation must raise money for him to sleep in a very good hotel and to feed him very well. If they can't meet all those requirements, he is not willing to come. He says 'I can't speak in small congregations.'

"That is pride. Jesus preached to a large congregation, but he also preached to one person. He went to Simon's house. He went to Zachariah's house. Yet He had thousands and thousands of people following Him. So when you say, 'I can't preach to this small group,' that's pride. That's very dangerous.

"We tell our pastors, 'If you have prepared a sermon to speak to a hundred people and you go and find you are talking to two people, preach as if you are speaking to a thousand people. Because God has intended it, to bring those two people for His purposes.'"

"Who knows if those are the only people God wanted to hear that message? What do you know will come out of those two people? And you may preach to 1,000 and only two are listening anyway." He laughed.

The Samaritan woman met Jesus when He was tired and exhausted, he tells the pastors.

"Then this lady came and saw Jesus. She was the only one there. With some preachers we have today, they would say, 'Here is only one woman, and she is not even my kind. I will not waste my time.'

"But Jesus, in spite of his tiredness, began to speak to this lady. And He preached to her. Eventually, the lady went to the town and said, 'Hear the man who has spoken about everything I have done.' All the people came down.

"We lose potential when we despise small numbers. We think, 'ah, there are only two people. I will not speak.' We need to have a unique ministry to a few people, not only a ministry for a lot of people."

"So, as for me, I believe in a big God who does big things, but He starts with small things and makes them big."

Chapter Ten

UGANDA: THE PEARL TARNISHED

"I realized, 'if I give bitterness away, I will lose nothing but I will gain much.' To the world, you look like a fool when you do this. But to God, a hero; and more than hero, a conqueror."

—Emmy Nnyanzi

It is astonishing to consider, as well, had not Emmy tamed his hatred of some of the most repressive regimes of the 20th century—that of the brutal, twisted megalomaniac dictator, Idi "Big Daddy" Amin and the corrupt regime of Milton Obote—PCM might have never come into existence. Or if it had, a spiritually crippled version would have been the result.

Immersed in anger and deep bitterness from the soul shaking-experience of social injustice, Emmy had learned to even hate the sounds soldiers of repression made; their language. Few Americans of faith, for instance, have suffered politically as Emmy and his fellow citizens have.

He explained this to the adults of Team 10 while traveling at night by car to Kampala. Walking alongside the bumpy, dusty and packed road were dozens of Catholic pilgrims. They were sojourning to a spot where Catholic martyrs in the distant past had met their mortal ends. At the height of oppression, from various regimes, there have been severe retributions to the different forms of the Christian message in Uganda.

The past 20 years "has been better," said Emmy.

"In the past we had bad relationships in all regimes between the army and civilians in Uganda," said Emmy, "because the armies used to oppress the people, not giving them peace. They could come and just grab your things because they have guns. They would not have to say anything."

The car bounced along the bumpy road, on through the dusty night. "Driver Emmy"—the full-time, professional driver for PCM—was keeping a close eye on all the pilgrims that occasionally spilled out into the road, some close to the car. Some had flags. Some carried crosses.

The Team 10 adults leaned forward, listening closely to Emmy's words, imagining the cruel, oppressive and brutal times many of the people they were seeing, had lived through. Many people had died during those repressive regimes.

Hatred soon followed pain and unresolved hurt, Emmy was saying.

"I grew up hating the language called Swahili," he said. I hated even hearing it because it was used by the army at that time and they were such bad people. Cruel. So whomever would speak Swahili, to me, had to be, in my mind, a bad person."

Emmy laughed at his former phobia.

"That was until I went to Tanzania and I found the people were speaking Swahili there, too. Then I understood; it's a language like any other language. But formerly, that was the bad people's language, the language 'they' speak."

"Now, I speak Swahili," he said smiling, shrugging as if it were simply another obstacle he had successfully overcome.

The simplicity of the resolution to his hatred astonished the Americans.

One said quietly, "Forgiveness really is the key, then, to healing these bad memories?"

"Yes, forgiveness," said Emmy, quietly smiling. "Can you imagine Jesus on the cross? People are spitting in His eyes. They are hanging Him on a cross, they have mocked Him; they have left Him naked. But He's just giving up all that, by saying 'Forgive them all they are doing, they don't know what they are doing?'"

"'They don't know?'" Emmy asked incredulously. "Can you imagine? They are hitting Him with a hammer, nails in His hands and feet and they "don't know?" Why did Jesus say that? It is because He chose not to think 'they intended this.' Many Christians are angry at people because they think 'they intended to hurt me.' Jesus blessed such people, saying they did not know. Shouldn't we do the same?"

The ability to speak the language of "the oppressors" that formerly made painful memories, but now through understanding and forgiveness brought peace, was a significant breakthrough on Emmy's faith journey. Such steps of deep reconciliation were spiritual signposts. He would be prepared to ask orphaned children to forgive their abusers, obtaining the peace that passes understanding by truly trusting Jesus.

The hum of the car's engine was the only sound as the men reflected on all Emmy was revealing to them about the depth of a truly spiritual life. Emmy finally broke the silence.

"Most Christians are so bound," Emmy said quietly, "because they think that if they hold onto bitterness and keep away from those who are hurting them, who are mistreating them and they just keep a distance from them, they will be fine. But even if you lock yourself in the house, that pain will find you there."

It is plainly seen that even believers struggle with bitterness," said Emmy.

"But if you are feeling sorry for yourself," said Emmy, "you will not receive the comfort of God, because you have already comforted yourself with your sorrow."

This is why, Emmy says, God reveals the pathway of peace by pushing people towards anxiety-free living, though it may look like foolish living to observers.

"One of the things people need to know," he said, "is that it's not all about us, but it is all about God. Jesus said, 'whoever wants to follow me must deny himself and carry his cross and follow me.' That is a very, very strong statement, a very strong message."

"Until we deny ourselves, we will be in pain. It's not easy to deny yourself but that's what God wants; to allow anything to happen to you for the sake of God. If someone tries to step on you, first think, 'what would Jesus do if He was stepped on? What would be His first reaction? Would He fight back or will he give His blessing on these?"

"And if He blesses those who step on Him, then that's why we are called Christians. We need to do that. And we don't lose much if we do that. It will save so much pain."

"Successful spiritual ministry depends on it." he said.

"The more you keep bitterness, you suffer much," said Emmy. "The more you allow it to go, then you gain peace. The more you live in peace, you can achieve much."

Emmy sees this principle in the mirror of his own life.

"If Jesus didn't help me and I didn't become a Christian, giving my life to Jesus Christ," he said, "I would be a very bad person. A very bad person. And I found good instead of bitterness when I came to Jesus, with my wife. That helped so much. So I knew that the only way we could save these children from being cruel to others, from being a big problem in this world and to also introduce them to Jesus Christ, was by bringing them and showing them love."

Emmy sees what he had been saved from.

"I realized, 'if I give bitterness away, I will lose nothing but I will gain much,'" he said. "To the world, you look like a fool when you do this. But to God, a hero; and more than a hero, a conqueror."

The test of rejection and bitterness is the place where many future ministries live or die. It may be the place God's hopes for mankind are murdered by the misery of hurt and pains unforgiven. For unless one forgives, God does not move.

The futures of Emmy and Sarah Nnyanyzi and Mark and Monica Barret would either be manifested or missed by a series of decisions set before the young school teacher in southern Uganda, out of sight of the rest of the world.

In fact, the destinies of hundreds of school children hung in the balance of what Emmy Nnyanzi would do when confronted with the horrors of his own past and what he saw as the obvious need to bring parental love to children such as himself.

If he made the wrong choices, those hundreds of children would have to wait for another to come to their rescue. The Barrets would have to wait for another opportunity to be the strength of a mission to save children's lives from despair. And in retrospect, who would have been the arm of salvation to those particular children, so happy today?

Who knows the threads of lives affected by so-called "private decisions" made in secret and announced to no one except to heaven itself? God surely does.

Chapter Eleven

TURNING AROUND

Mark Barret sat in his car in the driveway of his house. By the time he had driven home in a huff after throwing down "Surprised by Friendship" on his office floor, he realized he was making a mistake.

He sighed.

"What are you doing, God?" Mark prayed with his head on the steering wheel. He slowly got out and went inside, considering what was happening and how.

From the time he'd been filled with a presence at his childhood confirmation class, Mark knew his Father-God always had his best interests at heart. It's just that now things seemed so…out of his control. He was unable to make things happen the way he thought they should happen. To be honest, it kind of annoyed him; a feeling he tucked away inside him knowing it was not a proper perspective towards a loving Father.

He walked around the house, sat on the couch and wandered to the kitchen, opening the refrigerator door, staring inside at nothing in particular.

"Not hungry," he said, shutting the door hard. He ended up in his home office in his comfy leather swivel chair. He sat back and looked up at the ceiling.

"If God is leading me, and He is," said Mark, "then what am I doing here? I'm not listening. I'm not trusting. I'm not believing. How Christian is that?" he thought, falling silent.

Where was the man, he asked himself, who went "all in" when he felt something was right? When he played soccer as a kid with the best, winning teams; when he didn't waste time dating and finally found his life partner in college; when he started his medical practice to help a patient list of 2,500 kids and mostly when he decided to "give his life" to Jesus?

Mark had seen, and said "it's rare" to find believers who really went "all in" with God, and he'd always wondered why. God was so good. Now, here he was, being just that way. He thought of Paul the Apostle who "kicked at the thorns" from God.

He wasn't even close to what Paul had been going through and here he was, fighting God over…what? A blessing God was trying to give the family?

He thought of the title of the magazine article again, "Surprised by Friendship." What was he afraid of? Friendship? Not being the one who thought of Africa first?

The scripture, "For my thoughts are not your thoughts, neither are your ways my ways," floated through his mind in a confluence and collage of many thoughts, perceptions and concepts.*

"God is a God who loves to give his children surprises," Mark concluded. "What's the problem with that? I'm ready for it."

Mark sat up, slapping the desk decisively.

"It's not worth it—or smart—to fight you God. Sorry," he said simply and somewhat sheepishly, shaking his head and wondering about himself as he sometimes did.

He went outside, turned his car around 180 degrees and returned to the office, retrieving the article still sitting on the floor where he'd thrown it. The magazine was lying there quietly, thought Mark as he picked it up, almost patiently as if it knew somehow he'd be back to hear what it had to say to him. Nodding, he picked up what he knew would be the next step in his spiritual life. God was in control now.

He had a heart-to-heart talk with "Dad" on the way home.

"OK, Lord, you know Monica," Mark said. "You know what Africa means, more than I do. I trust you with my wife. You know..." and he stopped to consider what he was about to say and what it meant.

"You know I can't live without her," he finished up, nodding. "I trust you."

By the time he got home again Mark knew what he was going to say.

"OK, we're having share time," he called out when he walked through the door." He sat down with Monica, Libby and Bailey and explained how God had directed his day, reading the article to a surprised family. Then he summed up.

"What this means," he said to the wide-eyed, excited children, "is that your mom is going to Africa. Bailey, you're 11, so you're old enough to be in charge of the house. You're cooking and cleaning. Libby, I don't know what you're doing, but you're not misbehaving. You're going to help your sister."

"And for what reason we were doing this, we knew not," Mark said, recalling the decisive moment. "I mean, we just said, 'OK, go.' We were excited for Monica to go. Yet, we didn't know that Emmy and Sarah even existed. We just knew Monica was supposed to go to Africa."

---

*Isaiah 55:8

Chapter Twelve

DIVINE ENCOUNTER

---

*"Hearing him helped me feel really hopeful for one of the
first times in my life. I thought, maybe my suffering
had not gone unnoticed by God. Maybe God could help
me much more than I realized."*

—Monica Barret

Once in Mozambique, the excitement had worn off. A certain wariness and wondering where things had "gone wrong" seemed to replace the life-giving faith that had gotten her to Africa.

"I was seeing all the aspects of a dynamic ministry," Monica said. "But nothing really struck me as being the thing that I was supposed to do. There was just a sense that this was the wrong place for me. Something was not right but I couldn't put my finger on it."

"To make matters worse," she said, "God seemed to go silent."

Retreating to her living quarters to pray the situation through, Monica seemed to meet more resistance than relief.

"It was a real spiritual struggle to tell the truth," she said. "I spent a day or two in my hut reading the Bible."

As she read in the afternoon, she heard a sound. It was a plane and it caught her attention as if it signaled the arrival of something significant. On board the flight was Emmy Nnyanzi, who had come to see a friend and fellow preacher speaking at the ministry.

"Emmy's arriving was like a breath of fresh air," said Monica. He was just so full of the Word (the Bible) and God's love. He had a 'weightiness' about him, like the weight of the Lord. Everybody could see how much he loved the Lord.

When Emmy was given a chance to speak, Monica "connected" right away.

"He was so soaked in God's Word that everything he shared with us was like a big drink of pure, cool water," she said. "His heart was so full of compassion and sincere love. He gave his testimony and we were really moved. Soon we were all hanging on every word he said. There was something about the sharing of his childhood suffering that made our hearts connect quickly."

Giving away his bitterness had made him a strong man able to be compassionate.

"His stories of great suffering didn't seem to go with the humble, but strong man sitting before me," Monica said. "He was not hard or unhappy."

Hope returned to Monica.

"Hearing him helped me feel really hopeful for one of the first times in my life," she said. "I thought, 'maybe my suffering had not gone unnoticed by God. Maybe God could help me much more than I realized.'"

After the service, Monica had a chance to speak with Emmy.

"Somehow he knew I wasn't having an easy time. He walked over and gave me a verse for encouragement. Emmy's prayers for us were right on target with our lives because he was full of the Spirit. Things started changing in my life because of his prayers."

Emmy Nnyanzi would later say, "I had been wondering why God had me go to Mozambique. It cost more money than I had. There seemed little reason to go, except I felt I was supposed to be with my friend, Leon, who was speaking.

"But when I met Dr. Barret's wife and we talked and prayed, I knew she was the reason I had come. Out of all the people there, I knew we had met for God's divine purposes."

"I didn't understand that at the time," Monica said. "I just thought I had a very good friend that I needed at the time."

Nonetheless she called Mark. When she told her story, Mark knew what was happening.

"It was just so obvious to me; that's why she had gone to Africa," Mark said, "to meet Emmy."

Neither of them knew it, but Emmy was far ahead of both of them.

"He knew we were the ones to come alongside to help him," said Monica, "because he'd been praying about it for 10 years. He had God's vision of it."

"But he didn't tell us," said Mark. "Not yet."

When Monica returned home, Mark established an extensive "email relationship" with Emmy. A night owl, Mark would stay up late at night in email chat with Emmy.

"Emmy was pretty savvy when it came to computers," Mark said, "but his old keyboard was missing an "S" key so he'd have to figure out another way to spell a word if it had an "S" in it."

He laughed.

"Unbelievable. But we developed this long-distance relationship."

Mark learned Emmy had sold his house and his van "to feed a lot of kids." He was impressed with the courageous faith and wisdom of a man he'd never met, and the dedicated group of volunteer teachers following him in ministry to orphaned children, those who had no hope in the world.

"Soon," Mark said, "he was my closest friend, on another continent."

Chapter Thirteen

DON'T GO BACK

"Bubba's got the heart of a lion. He just won't quit."

—Gary Leventhal

"Hey, do you girls want to go skiing for spring break in 2008?" Mark called out to his daughters. "We could go to Colorado and have a great time."

It was only October but Mark liked to plan ahead. Sitting slumped on the living room couch, he figured he was going to need a break in the not-too-distant future. The medical practice was very busy. There were lots of patients to look after. Some snow sounded pretty good.

It was true; the family could have a great time skiing and that would have been fine. But God had something better, something more, for the Barrets than dodging pine trees or maneuvering moguls. A loving Father wants his children to have the best experiences, not just average ones.

Mark suddenly sensed the same still small voice that had told him to "go get the mail" and led Monica to Mozambique to meet Emmy was speaking to him again. Emmy had become a well-established friend.

Mark stopped thinking about a white spring break for a minute.

"Skiing, Lord?" Mark asked. "You know we would love this."

"No, no," the Spirit indicated to him, in that same familiar "voice" he'd felt before. "You need to go see your friend."

"What, Uganda?" Mark thought. "That's not a vacation."

But this time he was open to the inner promptings. No more magazine throwing. He reviewed how Monica had changed since meeting Emmy earlier that year; how Emmy had prayed powerfully into their lives through emails, phone calls, letters and whatever they could use to communicate.

"It's like the heart of God coming into our household when he contacts us," Monica said to Mark one evening, looking over his shoulder at the email chat going on between them. "It's just so healing and loving what he writes."

"I know it," said Mark. "I can't believe we know this guy. I mean, it's just amazing how we met him and what he's doing over there in Uganda. And the thing about it, no one seems to know about it—I mean, God knows about it, and Emmy's teachers know, but I can't get anyone here to really understand it."

The couple fell silent, recalling some of the reactions friends had to their new interest in Uganda and Emmy's work, Parental Care Ministries. Some had shown polite interest and moved on. Some didn't get it at all. Some had even discouraged them from "freelancing" in Africa.

"For the good of the Kingdom," they had said, "don't go back to Africa."

To their dismay the Barrets social circle soon dwindled as fewer of their friends found themselves interested in what Mark and Monica were doing and thinking; focusing their faith and time on a real mission from God, going "all in" in Uganda. It had been a disheartening time, a relational "pruning" time and even painful at moments.

But no matter what, Mark was determined they weren't going back to the way things had been before Mozambique. They'd come too far for that. They would hang tough regardless of invitations to parties, events and social gatherings—or none at all.

That pruning was a challenge, but even as a child athlete, Mark had heart to rise to a challenge. At least that's what one of his soccer coaches told Mark's father one day during a game.

Watching Mark compete and succeed with better players than himself, Gary Leventhal, from scrappy East End London, leaned over to Mark's dad one day at practice.

"You know, Bubba's got the heart of a lion," Leventhal said admiringly, calling Mark by his childhood nickname. "I really love watching him attack the ball. He just won't quit."

Leventhal's tenacity made a real impact on him, Mark recalled.

"Yeah, Gary was a wild kind of guy," Mark said, "and he had this patchy kind of hair thing going, like a dog bit him in the head. He loved coaching. I got to play for him, and with some of the best players in the South. That sort of makes a difference on how you do when you have a whole team of great players. You play harder, expect yourself to do better and, well, you win.

"Bubba" was familiar with team sacrifice and hard work. It had led him to 10 consecutive state championships in club soccer with three different states from the ages of 9 to 18 years old. One of these titles was with Coach Gary and the Germantown Thunderbirds in Tennessee.

"Gary's comment was one of dad's favorite things he ever heard about me," said Mark.

Now as he stared back into the computer screen waiting for Emmy's email reply, Mark remembered Gary Leventhal and the Thunderbirds.

"Look Monica," Mark said, "God has led us to a really wonderful guy who won't quit, no matter what. It doesn't matter what happened to him, what he doesn't have, who isn't helping him, who hurt him as a kid—nothing. He just keeps going for God and without bitterness. And he's playing with a great team."

He looked up at his wife who had shared so much pain with him, trying to figure things out.

"He's all in," said Mark. "How can we turn our backs on a guy like that? Does it really matter what anybody thinks or says about us? We just have to do what God is telling us to do, like Emmy is. He's the real hero. He's got the heart of a lion. We're not facing anything close to what he is and it's not stopping him."

"We can't," Monica said smiling, rubbing her husband's shoulders. "We won't. It's just wonderful when he writes. God is healing our hearts through him. We're finding the Father's love through him."

An email appeared from Emmy.

"Beloved," the email read. "We have been praying for you and that all is well with you and family and that one day you will come see us in Uganda. You are welcome here. Your friend, Emmy."

"That is so sweet of him," said Monica, her eyes misting at the thought of acceptance from people she hardly knew. "I see the "S" key is still missing," she laughed, wiping her eyes with her fingers.

While sitting on the couch months later, planning a spring break vacation, Mark recalled that he had been invited by his friends to come see them in Africa. He nodded, pursing his lips, in a decision.

"Hey, honey," Mark called out from the couch, "What do you think us about going to Uganda?

Monica, making coffee in the nearby kitchen, held her breath as she heard her husband's question.

"Wow, this is it," she thought as her heart began to race. "God is really doing something here with us. I didn't instigate this. It's all God's doing.'"

"As a family?" she called back nonchalantly.

"Yeah, all of us," said Mark. "I think it's time to go see them, don't you think?"

Chapter Fourteen

BREAKDOWN

---

*"The enemy really didn't want us in Africa for any reason.
There were times we were discouraged, perplexed and even
hurt...But I am amazed at how God weaves all those
things and makes things come out right—if you listen and
trust that you are hearing from Him."*

—Monica Barret

There is always resistance. Where there is little resistance there is little significance. The more life-impacting the work, the greater the cost—more than money—to start, maintain and propel it into the future. The greater the spiritual effectiveness, the deeper the spiritual apprenticeship.

Resistance takes many forms; mental, physical, spiritual. They can all be labeled 'the enemy' as an all-inclusive concept and lack of a better term. For Mark and Monica Barret, a smattering of these enemies became apparent as clarity slowly came to the depth of their involvement in Parental Care Ministries in faraway Uganda.

It was their ability to "hear" God that had brought them this far– and ironically their inability to hear that led them to nearly give up involvement in PCM, almost missing a nearly indescribable blessing God had in store for them.

The momentum of building and growth at Parental Care surges so rapidly today it's difficult to imagine the temptation to despair and give up that faced Mark and Monica early on. Yet obstacles and outright resistance were in their path from the beginning.

"The enemy really didn't want us in Africa for any reason," said Monica. "There were times we were discouraged, perplexed and even hurt by what people said or did to discourage us. But I am amazed at how God weaves all those things and makes things come out right—if you listen and trust that you are hearing from Him."

Physical obstacles, such as common transportation problems, presented themselves up front to the Barrets. But God "was there for them" they said when the family of four took their first firm step into a larger world, physically and spiritually in March of 2008. They were off to Africa on a mission trip not sanctioned, supported, organized or ordained by any mission-sending society, church or denomination. How did they do it?

"We were all convinced this was where God wanted us to go," said Monica. "He had led us step by step to this moment, letting us see Him put together the relationships over a period of many months. We had no doubt He would be with us now. He wasn't going to say 'Hey, you got it wrong, sorry!' and leave us hanging."

Still, there was some apprehension. Strangers in a strange land, they had little idea how they would be received by the children in Uganda. How would the at-large church community and culture in a country racked by poverty, war and pestilence in the not-to-distant past, receive them? Taking their young daughters with them was an extra step of trust in God in itself.

Mark, who is six-feet tall, had said, "It's one thing to go on by yourself and know you can deal with just about anything that comes your way. It's another thing to take your kids."

It was a walk into the unknown. No one could conceive what would happen or how they would handle it. The family took a deep breath and boarded the plane to Kampala, knowing that they would meet Emmy, Sarah and the PCM staff on the other side of the world.

"I just kept remembering, 'I didn't instigate this. It's all God's doing.'" said Monica, smiling.

The realization that God—not the mother—was the instigator of the family's first of many trips to Africa, would be a source of security when inevitable obstacles later appeared to discourage them.

The 10-hour overnight flight from London emerged into morning Ugandan sun high above stunning Lake Victoria, the source of the Nile River. Landing in crowded, nearly chaotic Kampala they were met by PCM's "Driver Emmy" in an old rented van.

"We got a hug, jumped into this old van and we were off for the five-hour drive to Mbarara," said Mark. "I kept seeing all these luxury vans at crossroads thinking, 'this is what we need for PCM.' I was already dreaming about the newer and better things we could one day have for the schools."

As the resources of a congested city slowly disappeared in the van's rearview mirror, the countryside opened up to a flat, green landscape that eventually evolved into miles of rolling hills. There was a lack of familiar 'Western' support systems—fast food, restaurants, hotels, or even speed limit signs. Speed bumps in the road forced drivers to slow down. The roads were outstanding in Uganda, but little else around them seemed to compare with that excellence.

Busses or even cars became scarce. People got around on motorcycles, "boda bodas," that grouped in gangs under roadside trees, waiting for up to three riders to cram onto crowded seats of a 90 CC motorcycle.

The affluence of the city evaporated, as city gave way to town, town to village, village to "hamlet" until all that was left was an occasional dwelling. There was a sense among the family that they were far, far away from home. Then, just two hours out of Kampala, the van suddenly, and noisily, broke down.

"Welcome to Africa," said Mark, laughing at the recollection. "There we were, a family of four stuck on the side of the road in rural Uganda. Here it was, the very thing we had been afraid of; getting stuck in the middle of nowhere."

To make matters worse the problem with the van sounded fatal, not simple, he said.

"The engine sounded like someone had thrown a wrench into it," Mark said. "We pulled over and there was nothing around us except some strip housing-shops. It looked pretty bad. At least it was still daytime."

Not knowing what to expect next, Driver Emmy "assured" them not to worry.

"All he said was, 'OK, we'll go get a guy'" by way of an explanation and disappeared into the buildings," said Mark.

Curious children slowly came out to peruse the Barret kids. A bench was brought out for the Barret girls to sit on. English is a language many in Uganda speak and use in school.

"But in this particular place," said Mark, in the green, gentle-hilled countryside, "it was not spoken very well."

No matter. Monica, Libby and Bailey sang songs to the children gathered around them. In the meantime, a repair gang was being formed.

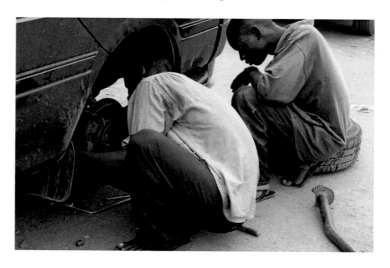

"And the next thing you know, three guys came out, got under the van, banged around and fixed it," said Mark, "It cost three dollars and, zip, we were on our way."

"God pretty much stripped all the fear away with the breakdown encounter," said Mark.

"We felt God was saying, 'don't worry about breaking down, don't worry about these people,'" said Mark. "They're going to love you and you're going to love them."

Chapter Fifteen

MEETING IN MBARARA

"We showed up. Sometimes, that's the most important thing you can do."

—Mark Barret

The hotel in Mbarara was "you know, OK" thought Mark, compared to Western standards. There were a few problems, such as black water coming out the bathtub faucet. The electricity went out from a windstorm "literally inside the hotel," said Monica.

But most of the problems were fixed readily. And the room was air-conditioned to bite off the high humidity that keeps Uganda green—when the power came back on.

Saturday night the family rested and woke up on Sunday in time for church.

"Wow!" Monica gushed, wide-eyed, and laughing as she picked out clothes from the big suitcases they'd brought, "Church in Uganda! Can you believe it?"

Holding one of the dresses she'd brought to the mirror, she said, "What does one wear to church in Uganda anyway?"

"I don't know," Mark mused, trying to get his camera gear together. "Medium, I guess."

"Medium?" exclaimed Monica. "What in the world is that?"

"I don't know, honey," Mark said, rummaging through a camera bag. "It's a poor area. Dress down a bit. Look, I'm wearing simple clothes. Say, have you seen my battery charger anywhere?"

"You're going to wear that?" she said in disbelief, "You look like you're going to the golf course."

"Hey, this doesn't look bad." Mark said, stopping, holding out his arms to his sides, "It's not like we're going to a parade or anything. You know, I think the charger is under the bed."

Monica looked at her husband collecting his gear. He was still tall and handsome she thought. She turned back to the mirror and held up a smart-looking dress, and shook her long dark hair out.

"But we're not going to 'dress medium' on our first Sunday in Uganda, are we?" she said to the mirror, and chose what she liked.

"I'm with mom, Dad." said Bailey, "Dress up."

"Me too," said Libby."

"Fine," Mark said to his family. "Do what you want. But you may feel funny when we get there."

As they came down the stairs to go, Emmy saw the family and nodded his head rapidly.

"Hello, hello," he said to Monica and the girls, nodding. "No, no," he said to Mark, shaking his head. "You must change."

He smiled again at Monica, Libby and Bailey.

"Change? Why?" asked Mark, surprised.

"Just change," Emmy said. "Quickly, so we are on time. Everything will be fine. Just change into something nice. Quick, please."

Mark dutifully did as he was told, shaking his head back in his room as he changed.

"Really, this looks fine," he muttered, "for a place that has black water in the bathtub."

As they drove out of town, they all noticed the houses became smaller and the roads bumpier. Large, green-leafed banana tress framed a blue sky. The strong sun on a Sunday morning was pleasant to feel, but too bright to look at for long.

Suddenly the van stopped. There was nothing around but a small Toyota pickup truck and a tree-lined road with no one on it.

"OK, let's get out." said Emmy, "Here, please. I want the four of you to get on this truck. May I help you up, young ladies?"

"What in the world are we doing, Emmy? asked Mark, "Where's the church? Did the van break down again?"

"No, no. Please get on the truck." Emmy said, "Here we go. Quickly."

"Why doesn't he tell us what we're doing Dad?" whispered Bailey as she was being helped up on the truck. "This feels funny."

Mark sighed, got on the truck and pulled Monica and Bailey up. The truck lurched forward and the four held on as it slowly moved forward.

"This is the nuttiest thing," muttered Mark. "Fully dressed on the back of a pickup. Now what?"

As the truck rounded a corner, the family saw what Emmy had known was coming; two long single lines of people on either side of the road, waiting for them to arrive. Dressed in their finest, colorful clothing, the men by the side of the road lifted their hands in the air. Women began to wave colorful pieces of cloth. A sound, almost a roar, began to fill the air.

"Wow, Dad," said Bailey almost shouting to be heard above the sound. "There must be a couple of miles of people. Look at them all!"

Human lines dressed in bright festive colors began to sing in unison and with fervent energy. As they lifted their voices high to the skies, Mark, Monica, Bailey and Libby beheld for the first time the sound that would remain with them all for a lifetime—the sounds of praise and utter thankfulness to Jesus.

As the truck drove between the lines of singing, smiling, clapping people, they fell into lines behind the vehicle, marching behind the Barrets, waving their hands in the air. The procession continued up the road, past pastors and their entire congregations; past officials and smiling children. It seemed as if joy and gladness was everywhere. As if God was smiling down on all of them.

The family was overcome.

Emmy, walking behind the truck with fellow PCM pastors, smiled his biggest smile yet.

"Welcome, friends, welcome." he said loudly. "These people have been waiting for you all morning. They want you to know they are so very glad you are here. That is why they are singing and praising their Lord"

"Why are they doing all this?" shouted Libby to Emmy. "We haven't done anything yet."

"You came," yelled Emmy simply, cupping his hands by his mouth.

As the truck rolled up to the church and the family got out, it seemed as if every person had to hug the Barrets, from the oldest to the youngest, smiling child. The people showered their fully accepting love on the visiting "friends" as they were called, welcoming them into their own family.

It was at this moment, Mark learned a valuable lesson

"It was the power of presence," he said years later, "We hadn't done a thing to deserve a reception like that. We hadn't even agreed to do anything. But we showed up. Sometimes, that's the most important thing you can do."

Chapter Sixteen

"YOU'RE THE ONE"

"This is just unbelievable. We've got to help these kids."

—Monica Barret

The next few days were head-turners for the Barret family whereever they went. Libby and Bailey played with children who hugged them without reservation, as if the girls were long-lost sisters. The joy of the PCM children, despite their circumstances, was infectious.

It was another beautiful sunny and sunglasses, deep-blue sky day in Uganda. A slight and refreshing breeze was blowing through the school grounds. The green hills sparkled and nature's elements seemed to shout out "life!"

It would have been paradise if the place was in America. A coffee shop would serve muffins and lattes in such a scenic setting—except Mark and Monica were finding that, in reality, circumstances were not all that good at the school.

They met with the teachers who'd followed Emmy and Sarah's heart in the ministry to children—without pay. There was simply no money to give them, Emmy explained, later. But they were not there for the money anyway, he said.

"We tell these teachers God will bless them for this work they are doing because we are all now planting a seed of love in these children," Emmy said to Mark and Monica as he showed them around the dirt-floored school rooms, empty now as the children played outside.

"The teachers are trusting that in days ahead, these children will become very important people to Jesus," he said. "That's because we have snatched them from all these ditches which devils dig to throw them in, so they can't finish because of their pain—from the disappointment which they have—that could cause them to make very bad decisions and die."

Emmy looked at the large group of playing kids. The school population seemed to be growing by the day. He smiled and waved his hand towards them.

"We tried to take care of the children ourselves, but there were so many and we couldn't handle them by ourselves," he said. "Then we brought in people to help us teach them."

"We had to tell the teachers, 'We cannot employ you because we don't have money to do that, but take it as a ministry. See it as a call from God that you have come to minister to these children and you are expecting your reward from God. We will be sharing the little we get with you, so that you can keep on doing this work.'

So that is what we told these teachers."

"How many teachers are there?" asked Monica.

"Eight," Emmy said. "Some have left."

"That was the toughest meeting of my life," Mark whispered to Monica after parting from the meeting with the teachers earlier in the day. "I mean, here is this group of dedicated teachers trying to help these kids, and they haven't been paid, ever."

"Did you hear?" Monica said. "He's got one teacher that has stayed with him for the last group he didn't pay. They just look so beaten down and discouraged. My heart just goes out to them."

Soon they saw the sleeping arrangements for the students. Most of the children were sleeping on the ground at night. As a pediatrician, Mark couldn't take what he was looking at.

"Monica, we've got to get these kids off the ground," he told her decisively that afternoon.

"I know," she said. "And you should see the food they're eating."

"Forget about the food," Mark said. "Have you seen the water? It kinda looks just like chocolate milk."

"They get it from the river that runs through Mbarara first," Monica said, shivering at the thought. "There are two water boys, Simon and Moses. They go down a steep bank with plastic jerricans. They said they carry them back up 45 times a day! I tried to pick up a jerrican full of water. They're really heavy. I don't know how they do it."

She shook her head at the thought.

"It's really dangerous down there too," she said quietly. "You could fall in."

"The conditions are heart breaking," said Mark. "It's because they have all these kids here. They started bringing orphans into their home in 2002 and had 41 kids living with them. Can you imagine? Then they sold their house and their car in 2004 so they could buy this property, and now most of these kids sleep on the ground."

"How many children live here?" asked Monica.

"About 120," said Mark. "If Emmy and Sarah still had their house…"

"Then many of these kids wouldn't have anywhere to live or anyone to love them," Monica said. "Emmy told us they'd die, remember?" she finished, her voice trailing off.

Mark and Monica looked around the small buildings that had been built with whatever materials that could be found. The cool breeze blew their hair.

"Is Emmy still getting paid teaching school?" Monica asked as she looked around through her sunglasses, searching for answers.

"No, God told him to go back to his village after he got saved in 1993 and start a church," said Mark. "They began everything in a mud hut. With eight women who didn't have jobs. He still teaches sometimes and gets money for food for the kids."

"Wow!" said Monica, falling silent again.

"Yeah, he and Sarah have been doing this a long time," said Mark, shaking his head, shuffling his feet in the dirt.

There was a contemplative silence as the sound of laughing children filled their ears.

"And get this," said Mark, looking up. "Emmy said they've been praying for their food each day. They've done it for a few years now."

"That's amazing," said Monica.

"Yeah. Emmy said they live by faith and that's how they kept going; by faith. He taught the children to trust God in every moment, every day."

Monica paused.

"How has that worked out?" she asked.

"Not bad," said Mark looking around the schoolyard again. "Emmy said in about 900 days they only went two days with no food at all. Most of the time they'd miss lunch, or breakfast, but not dinner—not going all day without eating. He'd get a side job, or a supporter would send money or a farmer who knew there were orphans here would come by. Things like that. Something would always happen to bring in some food."

Monica was astonished.

"What did they eat?"

"Oh, you know, nothing big," said Mark. "It wouldn't be much or very different foods, but at least some maize flour or beans. They'd live like that for a week and God would provide another thing and they'd keep on like that."

Monica took off her sunglasses, staring off into the distance not saying anything. It was too much to comprehend. She thought, "And the kids go to school eating like this?"

"Yeah, I know," said Mark who knew what she was thinking. "Can you imagine American kids thanking God for one meal a day of some beans and rice and being happy about it—or thinking God loved them? We think God has something against us if we can't have three meals a day of something really different. And that's just food. If we don't have the latest 'stuff' we're not sure God loves us at all."

Monica was stunned silent. She watched her well-dressed daughters Bailey and Libby who had not a material care in the world playing with happy children, who by American standards, shouldn't be happy at all. The clothes on the orphans were dusty and old. Most of the children were barefoot.

Mark followed Monica's gaze to the laughing children.

"Shoes and clothes, too," said Mark. "They need them."

"Not just any clothes," Monica said. "School uniforms. Sarah said all school children in Uganda have uniforms. If you don't have one, it's like you're strange."

"And desks and textbooks and, and, and..." Mark said ticking off a list that was getting far too long.

There was silence again.

"This is just unbelievable," Monica finally said. "We've got to help these kids."

"Yeah, I know," Mark said looking up into the sky. "I don't know what to do though. It's a whole lot bigger than I know how to handle."

Despite his large income and willingness to help as much as he could, Mark knew he did not have enough to provide these children with what they needed. It was beyond his ability to provide or even have an idea what to do next.

But God had a plan. It just wasn't what they expected.

After talking it over, they spoke with Emmy the next day. Sitting in the schoolyard on a few boards for seats, the two men talked about the future of the school.

"Look, I know some people who might be able to help you, Emmy," said Mark. "I've heard about his guy who really knows what he's doing when it comes to running non-profits. You need someone like him to help you raise money and get the things you need for the children; food, clothing, beds, books, clean water—everything."

"You know this man?" asked Emmy.

"No, I don't know him, I just know about him," said Mark. "I've heard a lot of good things about him. I think he's the guy, Emmy, really. He can help you."

Emmy was silent. He looked down and then around at the school of 120 children God had given him to take care of. As a boy, he tried living on his own strength to "pass through" tough times. As a Christian pastor, he had come to trust God in all things through years of "small beginnings"—to not be a "hireling"—even if it were a little, than trust a man who may promise a lot. He understood the difference in the character of a hireling who had skills versus someone with passion. Someone who had a heart.

He turned back to Mark.

"But, my dear friend," Emmy said, "this is not what God has been telling me. He is telling me that you are to be the spokesman for Parental Care Ministries."

"Me?" said Mark, completely surprised.

"Yes, I am sure of it," said Emmy. "I thought it when I met Monica in Mozambique a year ago, that the Holy Spirit had us meet for this very reason. That is why God took me to Mozambique, just to meet her, and then you. It was confirmed to me as we wrote back and forth in the emails all this time. God has chosen you to represent Parental Care in the USA. I am certain of it."

Mark laughed out loud.

"Emmy, I am honored you think this, but I can't do it," he said. "I have no idea how to run a non-profit ministry. I have no idea how to raise funds on the level that is needed here. I'm a doctor, not a non-profit organization executive director. I'm not qualified."

"God will show you, step by step, what to do," Emmy said, "as He has also done for us for years."

Mark looked down at his shoes and shook his head.

"I don't know, Emmy," he said. "I don't think so. It's…it's so much more than I can do."

If Emmy Nnyanzi has learned anything in 43 years on this earth, it is patience. He smiled at his "new" American friend he felt he understood so well, and was seeing for the first time. He felt like a brother to Mark; far beyond culture, race, geography and nationality. They were Christian brothers.

"Do what you think is best, my friend." Emmy said, in a reassuring tone, "but I think you are the one."

"OK," said Mark, shaking his head. "I'll keep it in mind."

The man who had been challenged by Daniel Wallace to "pray about it," and had thrown the magazine article on Mozambique to the floor, was being challenged in a way so much more than his limited expectations of himself, his learned skills and his own perceived potential.

It was a new era in trusting God for Mark Barret. It was not clear at all if Mark would meet the challenge, claiming all the blessings God had for and through him—or if he would turn away and give up, settling for second best.

Chapter Seventeen

DECEPTION

"We thought we couldn't do it. We thought it had to be someone else to take charge and lead the way. We thought we might fail at it, mess it up or make things worse...We didn't believe."

—Mark Barret

The eight days of meetings in Mbarara left the family deeply impressed with the character, approach and spirituality of the Parental Care staff and students. The next and more serious test came immediately upon returning home.

Despite Emmy's conviction that Mark and Monica were "the ones" to be the voice for Parental Care Ministries in America, Mark decided a "professional" needed to be hired to assist Emmy and Sarah. Mark wanted to ensure, he explained to Monica, the stability and expansion PCM was crying out for and to help the existing 120 children.

"And you know there are going to be hundreds more kids coming if Sarah and Emmy are funded," Mark said on the plane ride home. "Look what they've accomplished with so little. It's inevitable more children will come. We want the best for these kids, right?"

Monica stared straight ahead to the seat in front of her, deep in thought.

"I love these kids too much to mess it up for them honey," Mark said plaintively. "Look, how am I going to start a non-profit in Texas and run it while I'm a doctor, anyway? My boat is loaded. My plate is full. We need a paid guy who does this for a living, knows his way around and knows what to do."

"You mean a hireling, like Emmy told us about," she'd said, arms folded on the plane. "I don't like it."

"No, honey, I don't mean like that," Mark said, gently tossing up a hand. "Look, I know you believe Emmy's got the word on this and all—and I do too. He's a great guy. But let's be realistic. I have so much to learn when it comes to non-profits. It's too much. It's too hard to handle."

"Emmy said God would show us what to do," said Monica. "Each step of the way, remember? Start small and..."

"Yeah, I heard," Mark said, "'...and God will make something big out of it.' But PCM is big already. There are already 120 kids. Do you think Emmy and Sarah are going to stop at 120? No way."

Mark paused and took a sip from his airplane soda drink.

"Besides," he said, chewing ice, "Who do we know that will help us at home? Everyone thinks we were nuts in the first place just going to Africa."

Mark had a point there, Monica thought. Their social calendar had become next to nonexistent since Uganda was on their schedules. She wondered who would support them.

Monica couldn't even tell her father how wonderful the parade had been; or how sweet the PCM children were; or how the hearts of the entire family had been touched by the joy of the kids, even in their poverty. Monica had buried her father a few days before leaving for Uganda. Days after her return, Monica would find out her mother had inoperable metastatic cancer all over her body.

"I just get an uneasy feeling when I think of someone else coming in and taking over this ministry, when God seems to have brought it right to our doorstep," she said, and shuddered. "Especially with Emmy telling us, 'you're the one, you're the one.' He's pretty sure he's got the vision from God on that one. Either we trust him or we don't, is what I guess I'm saying. But do what you think is right. I'll support you."

"Trust me," said Mark, settling back in his seat. "This guy I'm thinking of? He's the guy. I'm pretty sure of it. He can do it. Yep. Don't worry. He's the one."

Mark had done the natural thing to do, the thing most good, organized church-going Americans might do; if you don't know how to fix something, find someone who does. Staff your weakness. The Barrets thought they found just the man for the job, whom they knew by reputation only.

A meeting was soon set up in a public place to introduce the new potential PCM USA director to the few friends following the Barret's progress. The man was experienced at nonprofit fundraising, appeared stable, seemed spiritual and was married.

At the evening meeting a month later, everything "seemed" to be going okay, thought Mark, as the candidate explained his expertise, what he had done and what he would do with PCM USA.

As the man finished his talk to the gathering, he came to sit next to Mark and Monica.

"That went well, don't you think?" he said. "Not bad."

Looking at the crowd, he leaned over and said confidentially, "Say, who is the blond in the third row?"

An electric shock went through Mark and Monica as they suddenly realized what was happening. Mark clearly saw how dangerously close he was to giving away a blessing God had reserved for him, Monica, Libby and Bailey; plus any volunteers who would follow them—and ultimately hundreds of orphans needing real hope, real love and real commitment to God's ways.

During the next two days, as the trio talked about vision, goals, spiritual life and dependence on God it became clear there was a chasm, a lack of understanding between them. The man may have been an expert at raising money but he lacked a similar spiritual edge that Emmy, his staff and even the children had honed to razor-sharpness. Could two men of such different viewpoints really work together? Or was it more important to have a heart-tie, a soul-knitting in purpose and desire to make God preeminent in all things?

"I think it's more important to work with like-minded people, people who pursue God with the same vision, than hire an "expert" who doesn't share a similar understanding," said Monica in a quiet, alone moment with Mark. "No matter what he knows how to do, I have a bad feeling about this working out in the long run."

"You're right," said Mark. "I'm sorry I did this. I wasn't trusting God at all. This was my way of fixing things and it's not working. Let's just tell him it's not what we thought it was, or wanted."

A few days later, the two were alone, slouched on the family couch once again, "back at the beginning." There was silence as they thought of the new responsibilities they were taking on.

"So, what did we learn?" said Monica.

"Oh my goodness, this lesson taught and showed us so much," said Mark. "Here we were; God had clearly called us to this ministry and we were actually trying to give it away. What were we thinking? I can tell you; we thought we couldn't do it. We thought it had to be someone else to take charge and lead the way. We thought we might fail at it, mess it up or make things worse. We didn't think God had made a mistake, but we thought it was a mistake for us to take it upon ourselves to do God's work. We didn't believe."

He looked over at his wife.

"I didn't believe," he said.

Monica smiled.

"So does that mean we're the spokespeople for PCM in America now?"

"Yeah, that's what it means" said Mark. "I think I'd rather believe we really can do all things through Christ Jesus, to do the things God called us to, rather than do something like this again."

He looked over at Monica.

"Sorry, honey," he said, leaning his head back into the couch pillow.

Monica looked at her husband who had listened to counsel about Libby's Christmas card; had gone back to get the magazine tossed on the floor; had sent her to Mozambique; had detoured the family from a Colorado ski trip to go to Africa and help orphans—and now was going to try something far out of his comfort range. She leaned her head on her husband's shoulder.

"I'm proud of you," she said.

"I still have so much to learn," Mark said, "but if we can learn to do the right thing, at the right time, with the right people, with the right heart-attitude ourselves then I think Jesus will be glorified and enable us to do this."*

"Hey, that's a pretty good list Dr. Barret," said Monica. "Say that again."

"I can't," Mark smiled. "I have no idea how I said what I just said."

---

*List courtesy of Joy Dawson

Chapter Eighteen

ALL THINGS ARE POSSIBLE

"We tell the children, 'As you are worshipping let it come from the bottom of your heart because you are showing the appreciation of what God has done for you, like King David... He came with a vision to worship God. If you don't come with a vision, you will not worship Him with all your heart.'"

—Emmy Nnyanzi

Mark was discouraged, worn out and tired. A few months after he and Monica decided that PCM USA was their task given to them by God and they could do if Jesus would guide them, it frankly appeared that they could not do it. Had they heard wrong?

The medical practice was booming—and was physically and emotionally demanding on Mark—but the PCM USA side of things did not seem to be coming together at all.

Coming home exhausted after work one evening and falling into his chair, Mark said to Monica, "We can't even get a church to talk to us, or hardly any other group. I wish I could just get into a meeting and make a presentation so we could even be turned down. At least we would be heard. We're not even getting that far."

The ineffectiveness of Mark and Monica's efforts to raise sponsors for the orphans seemed a crushing contradiction to Emmy's conviction that God would bring people to help PCM USA.

"And Emmy and Sarah are adding new kids to the school, it seems all the time," Mark said. "The school is growing but the budget isn't keeping up with them."

Mark sighed.

"We need money, honey," he said. "The school needs lots of help. The kids need to be able to eat."

"Jesus knows that," said Monica. "Let's pray about it right now."

"Jesus," Monica said, "Your name is Jehovah Jireh, 'our Provider.' You are our Provider. We lift up this ministry to You and its many needs. You know there are many—vehicles, food, salaries for teachers—and it is beginning to become overwhelming. We know You will provide for the work you have called us to do in Uganda. We ask for others to please come along side and help us with this ministry. We thank You in advance for Your provision. In Jesus name we pray. Amen."

"Amen," said Mark. "You know, the thing is," he mused aloud, "we're not connected to a mission-sending society, a church mission effort, an NGO, and PCM USA isn't even incorporated yet. We're just a mom and pop mission outreach. Maybe that's why no one wants to talk to us."

"Oh!" said Monica suddenly. "I almost forgot! Guess what came in the mail today?"

"What?" said Mark, smiling, trying to change his mood and look on the sunny side. "Donations? Love letters and advice?"

"No, better!" she said and ran off to the living room to get the mail.

"Better than a donation?" thought Mark. "This must be pretty good."

Monica came back bearing a large manila envelope stamped with a seal of the State of Texas on it. She pulled out a set of official looking papers and proudly handed them to her husband.

Mark looked at them for a minute, trying to comprehend what he was looking at. Suddenly, he sat upright in his chair.

"Are these the PCM USA non-profit incorporation papers?" asked Mark incredulously.

"Yep," said Monica smiling. "See? Signed, sealed and delivered."

"But...but that's impossible," Mark blurted, wide-eyed, holding the papers spread out in his hands. "I mean it's possible, obviously—here are the papers—but it's only been six weeks since we applied. No one gets non-profit status in six weeks. It takes months and months to get approved. This is unheard of."

"Jesus is amazing," said Monica.

Mark looked up at his wife. His mouth fell open.

"Do you know what this means," he said? "PCM USA is not a mom and pop mission outreach anymore. We can take in donations, process funds, give out tax-deductible receipts, everything. We're official now. This is great!" he said standing up.

"Yay, God!" said Monica. "All things are possible in Jesus."

"Possible!" said Mark, loudly.

"Possible!" said Monica even louder.

"Possible, possible, possible," they started saying together as loudly as they could and laughing, defeating the darkness of the day—until they suddenly saw Libby and Bailey leaning on the doorframe looking amused.

"You guys OK?" asked Bailey, smiling calmly. "What's going on?"

"No, no. No problems!" said Mark. "Hey, did you girls know that all things are possible with Jesus?"

"I've heard that somewhere before, Dad," said Libby smiling. "Oh, yeah, I remember; you've told us that all our lives."

"Well…I meant it!" said Mark. "All things are possible!"

He held up the sheaf of papers.

Listen, girls," he said. "See this? We're going to have a real mission to Uganda. And we're going to find sponsors for all these kids. And lots more kids! And volunteers will help us. Lots of them. And many denominations will join us not just one."

Monica held her hand up to her mouth, laughing, looking at Mark be excited.

"And we're going to get the kids shoes," he said, "and uniforms and textbooks and food and clean water and desks and…and…"

"And apples? said Libby, being lighthearted.

"And, apples, right!" said Mark. "We'll bring apples for all of them. And we're gonna hear those kids sing as loud as they can. Louder than they already do."

"I don't know, Dad," said Bailey, laughing. "That's pretty loud. They sing really loud already."

Thinking about Bailey's comment while sitting with his computer later that night, Mark remembered what Emmy had said during their visit, about the wonderful sounding worship of the children.

"We all tell the children that when you worship God, He comes and touches you," Emmy had said. "And when He touches you, you are healed. When you have a problem, the problem will go because God has visited you and touched you. And as you are worshipping let it come from the bottom of your heart because you are showing the appreciation of what God has done for you. So the children know when they worship God in Spirit and in Truth, God will be happy about that."

Mark began an email to Emmy—when it is 10 p.m. in Texas, Emmy and Sarah are just getting up at 6 a.m. in Mbarara—and told him how the miracle of the incorporation papers.

"Wonderful, beloved," Emmy typed back.

"I'm sure God will show us what to do now," typed Mark. "We prayed tonight to meet the right people who will believe in what we are doing."

"God will bring people to you," Emmy replied. "He will guide them toward you. Remember Monica came all the way to Mozambique and so did I? And for what? We did not know each other before. We did not know or understand God's purpose."

Mark pondered why it was so difficult to "rest" in God's purposes. If the Father knew what to do, why were they ever discouraged?

"How do you keep from being discouraged or anxious?" he tapped on the keyboard. "There is so much for you to worry about."

There was a long time to think as Emmy's reply was being typed out. Evidently, Emmy had a few ideas in the early morning sun of Mbarara.

Mark tried to guess what his friend would say after years of living in conditions he could not imagine himself surviving with joy. When the email reply came, Mark realized there was a lifetime of learning and a lot to think about in a relatively short letter. The application of scripture necessary to live Uganda was so different from what he'd ever known.

"When you start getting worried, that means you believe you will be the one to do that and help yourself," wrote Emmy. "But because you have failed to help yourself, there is no hope now. But once you have hope in God, have trusted God—when you find something which is beyond your own understanding, your own potential—you will just say 'Lord, take this,' and relax in Him and you trust Him to pave a way where there seems there is no way....it helps us remain in peace. That's why the Bible calls Him the King of Peace. He is the one who gives us peace."

"He also advises never get worried about anything, because when you get worried, there is nothing you can change...that's what Jesus said. You make the problem get worse, because you are worried."

"That's why Paul advises in Philippians by saying 'never be anxious for anything but through prayer and supplication let your request be made known to God.'"

What does that mean? Any problem which will come, you will just say 'Lord, I cannot manage this. I put this in Your hands; I put myself into Your hands; I put this problem into Your hands; be the one to help me.' And that will help you to relax and have your peace of mind."

Mark read the entire email twice. Then typed, "Lord, I give You Parental Care Ministries USA. Thank You for Your peace."

"Amen," wrote Emmy back from 10,000 miles and eight hours away, "Amen."

Mark was about to shut down for the night when he noticed something. He stared at Emmy's message and then smiled.

"You got your "S" key fixed!" he wrote.

The next day, Mark called Monica from work. The couple prayed again against any discouragement and for the provision the PCM Uganda children needed so badly.

"It's in your hands, Lord," thought Mark as he walked into his next patient room. A family was there, waiting for him. Mark was not prepared for what they would say.

"Dr. Barret?" the mother was saying, as the examination was over, "The Lord impressed us to give you a donation for the work you're doing in Uganda. The thing is, we thought God was telling us to double it in honor of Monica's mother who passed recently. So we made out a new check. Here you are, bless you," she said, handing them an envelope, and left.

Mark looked down at the envelope in his hand. Here was an encouragement from God of some kind.

"Probably a token of appreciation," Mark thought, happy for any sign at all there was support for PCM USA.

Ripping open the envelope, he looked at the check, re-reading the exact amount, looking for the decimal points so he would not be mistaken.

" There are too many zeros in this," he muttered, shaking his head. Then his eyes focused.

"This is for…$2,000," said Mark astounded. His eyes began to mist a bit. "This is $2,000 Lord. This is for $2,000."

Mark put his fingers on his eyes.

"Lord, you are too good," he said. "I bless your Name. I'm sorry I doubted."

He called Monica.

"Hey, guess what I have in my hand?" he said.

Never again would the two doubt that God could provide for PCM USA and the work they had been called to do.

Chapter Nineteen

PCM PURPOSE

"The children know that God is doing this.
And that the God who has done this, will do so much more."

—Emmy Nnyanzi

"The children didn't praise us for helping them.
They didn't see us as their saviors. They praised and thanked
Jesus for bringing their 'American friends' to help them."

—Monica Barret

"Emmy's coming! Emmy's coming to America!" yelled Libby Barret up the stairway of the house to her sister.

"What?" said Bailey running to the top of the stairs from her room. "Emmy finally got a visa? Thank you, Jesus!"

"Yeah, Dad said it's set," Libby yelled up. "Emmy will be here in May."

Bailey came running down the stairs. The family met at the bottom of the staircase, all smiles and talking at once.

"Wahoooooooo! Is Supermom coming too? How long will he be here? Can we take him to Maggianos in Dallas to eat his favorite dish, lasagna?"

"Wait, wait, wait!" Mark finally yelled above the fray, laughing. "One thing at a time. Here's what happened. Emmy got his visa on the fifth try. ('Alright!' the girls said). He's going to stay with us ('Of course he is' said Monica).

"Supermom did not get her visa, so she's not coming (awwwww) BUT, Emmy did say he can stay 20 days!"

"Oh, wow, 20 days," they all said. "That's great."

"Yeah," said Mark. "But listen; he's been to London and lived in New Zealand while he was at the School of Biblical Studies, but he's never been to America. It's going to be a whole other world for him."

"Oh, for goodness sake, he's got a computer," laughed Monica. "He's up to date."

They all laughed, but still, the family knew that making the transition from rural

Uganda to upscale Texas would be quite a jump.

How would he handle it? What would people think of him? What would he say to them? How would it go?

Wonderfully, as it turned out. By the time Emmy finally overcame difficult visa restrictions to visit America, Mark and Monica had organized nine team trips to Mbarara through the incorporated non-profit Parental Care Ministries USA.

Mark and Monica had an enthusiastic board of directors. Most importunately, they now had two staff employees. Justin "Deuce" Hayes left the biggest church in Tyler as a youth pastor to become the director of ministries for PCM USA.

His wife, Christie "Double Check or DC" Hayes, became the sponsorship coordinator and director of finances.

Teams of volunteers under the direction of Deuce and DC would soon provide much needed support for PCM USA and lead to many blessings which would soon follow in Uganda.

In 2008, $60,000 in donations came in. Then $200,000 in 2009; and in 2010, $500,000 in donations came into the non-profit entity Mark thought he could not run. Books, desks, shoes, uniforms, a clean water well, food and more were finding their way to Mbarara and beyond.

"By spring of 2011, there were more than 300 monthly sponsors for the children at $35 a month," said Mark. "More potential sponsors are inquiring."

"It had been a bit of a challenge at first," he said, smiling.

"Before our second team went out from PCM USA in November 2008," said Mark, "we were just praying so hard for that first person, that 'someone' to come and give us that legitimacy we needed so badly."

After receiving an unexpected email asking him about PCM, Mark had made a lunch appointment with Jay Ferguson, the headmaster of a local Christian school. Mark was hoping to somehow convince Jay to consider coming to Africa to see PCM, meet Emmy and Sarah, the children, and see for himself how God was working there.

"What we really needed at that point was to have someone—that one person—come alongside and really believe in us," said Mark. "We needed all the encouragement we could get. I was hoping hard Jay would be that person."

What he didn't know was Africa was in Jay's heart already.

"I was so nervous before we met, and I had all my arguments laid out in my head, ready to convince him to come," Mark recalled. "But even as we were sitting down, the first words out of Jay's mouth were, 'So, Bub, who's going to Africa with us?'"

Mark was floored.

"The Spirit had already spoken to him. I didn't have to say anything. I was so happy. It was such a boost to have someone like Jay come on board to help us, right when we needed it."

The children at PCM Uganda had a proper perspective though, as nine teams rolled through the schools, upgrading the lives of the kids.

"The children didn't praise us for helping them," said Monica. "They didn't see us as their saviors. They praised and thanked Jesus for bringing their 'American friends' to help them. Then they thanked us for coming when Jesus called. A big difference. They are still depending on Jesus, not us."

"That's the entire point of the ministry to the children," said Emmy, during a PCM Vision Dinner of about 250 donors in Texas. "And if that point was missed," he said, "so was the real meaning."

"Our major goal," Emmy said, "is to let people know about Jesus, to know about God. The work we are doing is giving the children education which is very good, but without Jesus, it will be useless for them."

"That observation was based on experience," he said.

"We have seen so many people who have been educated now in Uganda, but because they don't have Jesus, their life is a total mess," he said. "They are so confused, we've found that their education has not benefited them at all. We find someone who is not educated but with Jesus is better off than that."

"Another thing, we know that we are here (on earth), but only on a temporary basis. Our destiny is in heaven. So whatever we are doing, we should prepare people for tomorrow, to be prepared for heaven. That is the major reason why Jesus came to this world, so that we may have eternal life. Because if that is not the case, then we would be in a hopeless life because of one thing; we all know we are going to leave this world, whether we are ready or not. We want the children to depend on Jesus, not us. If anything should happen to me, I want the children to know and be sure that Jesus loves them. They know this, for sure."

He leaned over the lectern and smiled. He had everyone's attention.

"The children know we are not permanently here," said Emmy. "So if we take evangelism out of PCM and just give them material things, the things for today, we have not benefitted them at all. But we need to use education for kids to reach out and speak to people so that they may know Christ—because that's our destiny. He is the way, the truth and the life. And that's what we need. We need to give people life! If all we do is just a "humanitarian" effort without showing them their destiny, then we have not reached our goal."

Emmy paused and looked around the room. His time in Texas was almost at a close. He'd met and prayed for many people, been taken many interesting places and been received warmly in all his speaking engagements. Soon he would leave America and all its wealth behind and return to Africa. He wanted to impart a blessing to his new American "friends."

Emmy knew he had only one thing to give; Jesus. The parental love of Jesus was all he ever had to give to the children at PCM, to Sarah, to the teaching staff, to the gathering in front of him. He knew the tenacious and ever-present love of Jesus was so much more than anyone expected.

"When you saw our PCM children worship in the video tonight, did you enjoy it?" he asked.

There was wide assent.

Emmy said, "One time King David told his wife, 'It was God who put me over your father's house and yet I was nobody. So when I remember that, I cannot fail to dance before Him as a sign of giving thanks for what he did for me.'"

"So that's what we tell the children, too. 'You need to have a reason when you come before God; that's why you worship Him; that's why you praise Him.' And for sure, they have a reason. Always have a reason to worship Jesus, and God will come to you."

"And what is the point of the children living there at the school? We tell them, 'God will come to sleep with you.' So they have a reason to hope. So do you. God will come to sleep with you."

"One of the songs the children sing is called, 'Now I See the Vision Coming True.' Do they have hope for the future?"

"Of course they do. 'First of all,' we tell them, 'by working with what you have.'"

"But now they are seeing His provision; they are seeing God is moving them from one step to another; they are at school like all other children. They would be hopeless if they didn't have someone who cares; but now they have people who are caring for them, even you; all you friends who are helping them to grow. God will bring friends to help you, just as the children have been helped."

"One of our boys, is called 'Good Sir.' He approached my wife one day, and she saw him smiling, smiling, as he came to her."

"'I want to give thanks to God," he said to her. "When I see myself also going to the school, it makes me cry sometime because of joy. Sometimes people see me not talking very much. It is because the joy becomes beyond words to say, so I just kept quiet. I wanted to tell you this."

"Tell somebody and give thanks to God for what he is doing for you," Emmy said. "It will give you joy."

"The children know that God is doing all these things for them. And that the God who has done this, will do so much more. They believe Him more. That's why they have hope. I know they do. You can listen. You can hear it when they sing to God. That is your hope too."

Web Extra: See the PCM video the "Power of One" at http://www.youtube.com/watch?v=4j6U8UsAOtI

Chapter Twenty

KATYAZO PARADISE

"He's got my mind, my heart, this whole ministry.
I'm just never going to let it go until the day He calls me home."

—Mark Barret

Starting PCM USA took a combination of God's encouragement, will, courage—and heart. Locating sponsors for orphans; raising funds for bunk beds, uniforms, food, clean water, education and teachers; finding drivers, building new classrooms, purchasing new properties and pushing through a vision of a future for the kids was a full-time job in itself.

"God has prepared me my whole life for this moment, for this time, in Africa," said Mark, standing on hillside overlooking the breathtaking 68-acre PCM Katyazo (pronounced Kat-Yah-Zo) property in Uganda.

Mark had led Team 10 to the property site of the new PCM school, which was the gift of a single donor. As the team wandered awestruck at the serene qualities of the pastoral property, white puffy clouds drifted over lush, green nearby hills in splendorous, gorgeous scenery usually reserved only for the very wealthy. It is fitting that the 'least of these'—orphans—will live and praise their heavenly Father for His blessings in this fabulous setting.

Bulldozers leveled the earth as trees were cleared away and tilapia fish ponds were filled with water. A 14-acre bean and cornfield was sprouting and a large banana plantation was bearing fruit.

Soon, hundreds of orphans would be laughing, singing and becoming the salt of Uganda—and perhaps of Africa and the nations, as they grew in trusting God.

"We will be building a senior high school here first, opening in January of 2012," said Mark, pointing out places that building plans were being carried out. "Senior students will go to class in that area in front of us, as well as work the farmland behind us for bananas, beans and corn. The site will hold dormitories, classrooms, a library, a church and multipurpose gathering room and eventually a primary campus for the elementary-age children.

"We hope to have 1,000 children running up and down this hill at Katyazo soon. We will have fields to run in and fields for soccer and netball games. One day this will become home base for PCM Uganda complete with several guesthouses and even a health clinic for the local villagers."

He paused and took a deep breath of the fresh air, taking in the ascending scenery.

"It's just really a blessing to have a heart for God, to have a heart for doing what you love doing," he said, "loving on kids who are just...so loveable." And he laughed.

That particular day had seen Mark photograph stacks of smiling kids outside at the 4-acre dirt school grounds in Mbarara. PCM staff in Texas would soon post or otherwise distribute the photos for sponsors. Hundreds of kids were already sponsored with more about to be sponsored. Mark had joked, laughed and made light-hearted remarks to each child all afternoon, getting them to smile their best grin and taking photos until the sun went down in golden glory. Whatever dire impression the economic situation makes, the kids find themselves in a pastorally beautiful setting.

The children, in clean, "pressed" uniforms, smiled shyly, somehow seeming to reveal their best inner selves as the sun slowly created a golden glow behind them.

"Say, 'seka' (smile)," Mark would laugh with the children. It was a family fun time...with a family of 300!

That night, the team made a real movie available—along with popcorn and Coke for each child, on a big screen he had brought for the occasion, as well as a real popcorn popper for popcorn.

Almost ironically, at the equator where it never snows, the movie shown was the animated film "Ice Age."

"I have no idea if these kids even know what snow is," said Mark out of the side of his mouth as he watched the children's eyes glued to the screen. "I think this is the first movie many of them have ever seen, much less with Coke and popcorn."

Mark had said to the PCM staff in Mbarara, "I just want them to experience what we take for granted at home. Every child should go to a movie with popcorn and a Coke at least once."

Wide-eyed children waited curiously to get their bag of popcorn, wondering what it was they were going to eat. There was a sense of cultures colliding, as kids ate the airy, puffy corn and laughed at how light it was in their hands. They loved it. Simple comforts and pleasures overblown to near-hedonism in developed nations have yet to be tasted in innocent simplicity by many in the world.

In an age when the "Jesus" film tours the remote parts of the world, popcorn, Coke and a fun movie may seem superfluous and a missed opportunity. But PCM children already know Jesus, and in ways nearly unimaginable to many believers.

With the Gospel already living in the hearts of the children, it was not necessary to show the Jesus film—but popcorn was such a special experience that Emmy asked the kids to stay after the movie to make sure "all their brothers and sisters" got a bag. Underestimating the popcorn needed to feed such crowd, the movie was over before all were fed. The Texas team manned the popcorn maker for an hour later until all had some.

Looking out over a few hundred children in the outdoors night, sitting quietly while waiting patiently for popcorn was a scene in contrasts. Would American kids stand for the wait, the simplicity of popcorn or the idea of hanging around until everyone was served?

"Whatever is at work in these PCM children is needed in America," said Team 10 member Rocky Gill.

On Sunday at the outdoor service at PCM, guest speaker Gill would say to the 500 gathered people, "I call Uganda heaven on earth. Don't wish for what we have in America. We are spiritually sick in many ways. We want what you have here."

"Yes, God has prepared me for these kinds of challenges all my life," Mark said after the movie, "and I've learned so much about patience from these children." He leaned in as if to confide and almost whispered.

"It's amazing. They almost never get angry—really, I haven't seen it—they're never upset when something doesn't happen. They just roll with the punches and whatever happens is what they do. It's incredible. I'm a pediatrician. I know. Kids just don't do this."

"Though it has been stressful at times," said Mark, "it has been very reward-ing following the leading of God who knows even better than we do what will satisfy us."

Laughing, he said, "I just couldn't ask for anything better. What could be better than this? I don't know. God has given me the desires of my heart."

"And Jesus will do that for others. That's what I want people to know," said Mark. "He will do it for you. At the response of the heart is where it all happens. It's all about the heart, not about the head. If you can get to someone's heart, you've got them. He's got my mind, my heart, this whole ministry. I'm just never going to let it go until the day He calls me home."

Chapter Twenty-One

THE ROAD TO RWEMIKOMA

"This is the experience of unfiltered love."

—Rocky Gill

"The children who need us are here in Uganda. They are the ones God has brought to us for His love and care and to introduce them to Jesus. What would I do in America?"

—Emmy Nnyanzi

As Team 10 went "off-road" one mildly rainy day to remote Rwemikoma—though most roads in Uganda are unpaved—out to the PCM School set in green, lush and tropical hills dotted with banana plantations, the much less well-off segment of society emerged. Mostly subsistence "diggers" (farmers), these were people who would be described in the West as the "one paycheck away from poverty" types—but who had never had a paycheck in their lives to begin with.

Bright sun intermittently broke through rainy conditions seeming to set the landscape on fire with an almost otherworldly brilliance and a misted rainbow effect. Comfortably ensconced in a Land Cruiser provided by PCM, it was almost easy to forget that locals traveled by bicycle and walking, not having the luxury, perhaps to be in awe of the spectacular landscape provided on a daily basis by the artist, God.

There was a stark sense that life itself hung in the daily balance of often cruel economic circumstances in these emerald green hillsides. The feeling covered the scene like a scrim over bright theater lights, bathing the beautiful sunny stage before us with shades of gray, creating a nagging feeling of foreboding. It was absolutely gorgeous on the road to Rwemikoma. Any Southern California land developer would die to have access to such scenery to install the next "Starbucks" or trendy fashion mall-hotel-concert-restaurant complex—if only it weren't in Africa!

The reality of the remoteness of Africa and reflective quiet set in as the team travelled "further out" Mark said, than many PCM groups from America. Sarah Nnyanzi makes the two-hour trek from Mbarara at least twice a month, sometimes more. Sometimes "teacher Jonathan" goes in her place. The skills of Driver Emmy and the other staff drivers are needed to navigate the tricky roads to the high jungle-like outback to get her there and back. When it pours down rain, as if often does, water creates deep road-ruining rivulets that can "wreck a car like that," said Driver Emmy with a wide smile, snapping his fingers and laughing as if it were just part of life—which it is.

It is good locals are so understanding of the life structure people rely on in places such as Rwemikoma. It would be presumptuous for visitors to think they could grasp the realities these people daily lived in, and the spiritual strength required to surpass the circumstances.

Though Mark said Sarah is as passionate about the children as her husband, "Supermom" saves her speaking for the children on whom she keeps a wary and cautious eye. She knows the realities many of the children come from are nearly unspeakable and the kids need constant supervision.

"Well-meaning visitors from the West could easily endanger a child's stability with too much attention, or even what seem like simple gifts," she said. The Nnyanzis ask contributors and sponsors not to send too much to the children they support.

Chinese engineers were present as we passed on wide muddy paths. They were surveying the red-clay tracks for future road construction, said Sarah Nnyanzi.

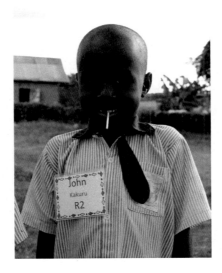

Asked about them, she said, "There are many Chinese people among us. They are always working on the roads." Asked if she minded the presence of Chinese communists in her country she became thoughtful.

"Since they are here, we can talk to them about Jesus," she finally said.

The PCM School in Rwemikoma is not as well supplied as its counterpart in Mbarara, but the staff, led by headmaster Daniel Mutungi is just as dedicated and paternal towards the children in their charge. Day students only, the almost 200 children in Rwemikoma come for hours of instruction. But lacking supporters, they do not eat lunch.

Yet the lack of food did not seem to diminish the enthusiasm the children had for their visitors, or the obvious joy they had in playing organized games with the teenagers from America in the hot sun.

The Rwemikoma School is special in what God is doing far away from the eyes of men, maybe even more than in Mbarara. The school is so removed from the beaten track there is no way or reason anyone would stumble on it by accident. Only intentional visitors come to Rwemikoma.

That being the case, there is little "trickle down" from a nearby affluent town, industrial surplus or even wealthy neighbors. Visitors from a foreign land are a treat, and the children seemed to view it so with incredible interest.

The welcome by the children was so effusive, one team member said, "This is the experience of unfiltered love."

Fresh drinking water has been a constant problem in Rwemikoma. It must be "biked in" by a youthful water porter, who earns about two dollars a day bringing gallons of muddy rain or river water to students.

The Barrets and the U.S. Supporters of Parental Care have attempted to bring in a well to the school and bring relief. That effort failing, a single Sunday School class in America sponsored lunches for the students for an entire year!

"I know why the well didn't work," said Mark Barret, to the gathered children in neat, lined rows before him. "God wanted you all to have lunch for a year!"

During an astonishing display of joy and gratitude, a student, Joshua, was chosen to pray for their first lunch. The passionate lunchtime prayer lasted more than a minute with a hundred hands up in the air, arms outstretched and faces turned to heaven in prayer and praise, as words of thanksgiving tumbled out in English and whatever dialects the children knew.

Afterwards one inspired adult team member inquired, "Who is Joshua's sponsor?" Finding he had none, he exclaimed, "Well, he does now,"and became the child's sponsor at $35 a month.

Crowded under the shade of a large tree to escape the rainy humid heat, lunch was served by PCM America staff. Dessert was a green apple, a rare treat that many children held high with big grins on happy faces. It was only the second time in their lives many of these children had a green apple.

Watching the unfolding expressions of joy, it was difficult to imagine how any of these children would have been reached with the spiritual comfort of Christ—or with the hope of education—unless indigenous ministers such as Emmy and Sarah had found, reached out and were determined to touch lives. God's determination to reach the lives of those "far away" was being shown before the eyes of Team 10 through the efforts of the founders and staff of Parental Care.

It is hard to conceive of a more worthwhile endeavor, or the worthiness of the effort being made right now in places such as Rwemikoma or the PCM School in Ibanda, and the PCM facility being built at Katyazo on the 68-acres of pristine property. Schools at remote Kyasenya and Minekye have recently started.

Emmy has no plans to stop taking in children regardless of how many he has now. Since his first trip to overly-affluent America, he was asked if given a choice, would he live in America or Uganda?

In typical "Emmy fashion," he did not answer right away, carefully considering the question.

"Here." He finally said, and fell silent. It is odd how really secure saints of God don't seem to feel the need to over-explain their position, theology or vision. Emmy has no "sound bites" to rehash, no patented explanations, no name-dropping and no desperation to get "publicity."

God was in charge of his life, he explained.

"Here is where God has called me." Emmy said calmly, "If I were to go to America to live, it would be very nice, yes. But I would not be doing what God wants me to do," and fell silent again.

Thinking a bit, he added, "The children who need us are here in Uganda," he said, smiling. "They are the ones God has brought to us for His love and care, and to introduce them to Jesus. What would I do in America?"

Mark Barret said, "That is the reason my best friend is a black man in Africa; his heartbeat and mine are the same for the children and for God."

Chapter Twenty-Two

THE CRUCIBLE OF REJECTION

*"Until you go and see and hear for yourself, it's all just words.
How do you explain the presence of God?"*

—Mark Barret

Many returning volunteers with PCM teams in Uganda say something similar to, "I saw real love" or "They have real faith over there." Most seem to say, "The children really worship the Lord," or "This changed the way I see God."

Many end with the refrain, "You just have to go," accompanied with big smiles, or the shaking of heads. Few seem to find the words to explain themselves adequately.

It was in Africa, perhaps 10,000 miles from home, that "home" was finally found for Monica Barret. It was an African man, Emmy Nnyanzi that helped Mrs. Barret find her way from rejection, hurts and wounds to her Father's house, just as he had years earlier.

Both were fired in the crucible of rejection and wounds from those close to them.

Both sought God for relief from their rejections, even cruelties they had attracted from supposedly safe environments, penetrated by slings and spiritual spears of disdain.

And both made choices resulting in hundreds of youngsters in Uganda achieving much more than a mere semblance of the parental love Monica and Emmy found lacking in their own youth. If they had not achieved, persevered, plundered the enemy's camp and disarmed the spiritual weapons formed against them, none of the remarkable achievements of Parental Care Ministries would ever have come into being. Monica would not have gone to Mozambique and met Emmy.

The lesson is sobering. How many poor in the world go without the comfort and relief that might be afforded them because the providers are "taken out" by concerns, worries and wounds of this world? How many may share a remarkable destiny similar to Mark and Monica Barret—who transcended their lifestyle to find strength, purpose and even love in a remote, undeveloped country—but are distracted or derailed from their adventurous destinies because of the bondage of bitterness and unforgiveness?

The keys for breakthrough were a combination of faith, prayer and "stepping out" with God by hanging on to the idea that God was "good all the time" while simultaneously scaling obstacles put before them and not letting go.

Once the Barrets were convinced it was God talking to them about Africa, they put all else aside—friends, social life, the acquisition of goods—and concentrated on one goal; full obedience to a living God leading those who seek Him to a land they do not know, for a purpose they can't understand until they get there.

The fruit of their endeavor has been a full transformation in their lives. The persistent pioneering efforts by the Barrets, adding to the ground-breaking work by Sarah and Emmy Nnyanzi, has also swept in hundreds of the Barrets neighbors, friends and co-workers in the moderately-sized town of Tyler, Texas.

Teams of short-term supporters have sent themselves to Uganda and returned with a vision of love many can't adequately explain as they simply smile at the recollections of their journey.

Mark Barret has all but given up trying to articulate the experience.

"Until you go and see and hear for yourself, it's all just words," he said. "How do you explain the presence of God? I've learned so much from the people in Uganda. They have true faith, a faith that makes ours pale by comparison."

Chapter Twenty-Three

THE "MOST OF THESE"

"I never get tired of coming here. I never will."

—Bailey Barret

In the hot Ugandan sun, Mark—called 'Epa' by his African friends—shielded his eyes and studied a traffic ticket Driver Emmy had just handed him for "too much cargo" in a small truck. The PCM dump truck had just carried bunk beds for 20 children to the PCM School in Ibanda.

The beds were paid for courtesy of another Sunday School class in Texas. They were finally arriving at their destination when police intervened on the happy convoy.

"I am sorry, Epa," Driver Emmy said. "Our truck looked very smart going down the road today. Many people were looking at us, wondering who we were. I suppose the police looked too."

Epa knew the fine meant spending rent money the school facilities needed—the four classrooms and two sleeping rooms plus the entire compound. He squinted reading the words.

The fine was for 40,000 Ugandan shillings.

As the beds were being set up on the dirt-floor "dormitories" a tall, slender young man and smiling young woman slid in beside Mark and looked over his shoulder at the paper he held.

"I am so sorry this happened, Epa." said Hope, the head teacher of the school, in a soothing voice as she looked at the ticket.

Abson, the headmaster of the school shook his head as he read the writing out loud.

"Hmmm, I see the fine is equal to four days rent for our entire school and living compound," he said. "Too bad."

Epa calculated the fine in American dollars.

"Yes. I see this ticket is for 16 U.S. dollars." Epa said, looking up and smiling. "I think we can handle that. Best fine I ever paid for in my life!"

Abson and Hope laughed and walked away to talk to excited students about to get something very special—a bed.

The bunks had been delivered by PCM Team 14, and now were being assembled and put into the two student rooms.

John VanDyke, a volunteer from Michigan maneuvered the bed into the tiny space.

"It's amazing we can even get the beds in here," John said, making the room fit the bed, not the other way around.

But the payoff was excited children. Team 14 and PCM USA were determined to get as many children as they could who were sleeping on the floors, into beds. And as soon as the beds were in place, smiling children sat on them, giggling with joy.

Rich and Page Wolowski, also volunteers from Michigan, stepped back to watch the kids who seemed to be in total peace, sitting on a real bed in the tiny closet of a room. One child, named Immaculate, smiled broadly as she covered her smile with her hands.

"This is unmistakable joy," they said to each other. "It doesn't get better than this."

"We would like to sponsor Immaculate!"

Epa walked over to the rooms and looked at the living spaces where the bunks were going. He saw uneven dirt floors in tiny closet-like rooms and wondered if he would be as thankful if he were sleeping in such a place. Somehow he doubted it as he considered the many items—entertainment, food, possessions—he "required" in life to make him content. He saw afresh how just a little made the children very happy.

"I know I couldn't live that way now and I don't think I ever could," he mused. "And the food they eat—it's always the same. No options. Porridge in the morning; corn meal/potato mix with beans at lunch. Day after day after day."

He shook his head at the thought of a permanent reality he would be powerless to change.

"I just couldn't do it," he said to himself. "It's a challenge for me to eat the same thing two meals in a row."

In his mind's eye, he saw the children when they got their first green apples in their lives here at Ibanda.

"It makes so much sense why you'd treasure any variety to your diet," he thought, "a simple apple. I understand now why you would eat this treat down to just a few seeds."

His thoughts challenged him. Why couldn't he be thankful like these children— "the least of these"—whom he was serving? What was missing from his life that he could not be content in all circumstances as these children were?

He turned and watched Salfine just 8 years old, who had just received her new bed. The small, PCM-uniformed girl was organizing everything she owned in the world in a small box at the foot of the bed. What could she have that was important enough to keep, he wondered? He'd find out.

"Hi." said Epa. "Well, do you like your new bed?"

Salfine's wide smile was her response. She was very grateful. Rich and Page sidled up to share in the joy. With the three of them present, Epa was a bit bolder.

"Say, may we see what you have in your box?" he asked, indicating all of them.

Shyly nodding, Salfine opened her box. The trio realized the girl's entire life was opened before their eyes, everything she owned, everything that meant anything to her. As she revealed her possessions, Rich, Page and Epa drank in what they saw—and learned.

Salfine had a few shirts, two skirts, some moisturizer, a towel—and a letter from her PCM sponsor in America taped to the upper part of her box. It was a short note of encouragement sent a few months earlier—along with a pink "Beanie Baby." Salfine smiled brightly for a photo to go to her sponsor.

That was the extent of her worldly possessions.

"Webale (Thank you)," said Epa, smiling and the three left Salfine with her new bed.

"That was amazing." said Rich, as he left, "That was all she had."

"You could tell she thought the world of the letter," whispered Page. "Thank you God that someone sent it to her."

Mark went back out to the school courtyard, where bunk beds were still being as-sembled amid laughing children. This was a time to ask God, he thought, what was really going on? What was being revealed in his own life and the lives of those he'd come so far to "touch."

"Maybe, just maybe we have it wrong when it comes to understanding who 'the least of these' are," Epa mused to himself as he watched the happy, joyful kids in front of him.

Thinking of his home and well-to-do city in beautiful East Texas, he fell into reflective comparison, as he often did when visiting Uganda.

How could such a life-giving spiritual reality exist in Uganda, on the same planet, calling on the same God, spirit and faith, and yet be so different from what he experienced at home? It was his 8th trip to Uganda and he was still amazed at what he was seeing. It seemed on every trip, he'd asked questions in prayers, "What God? What are you showing me?"

He was surprised this time when he suddenly heard a voice cut through his thoughts.

"Dad, what are you thinking?" asked Bailey. She put her arm through his and looked up into his face with calm, questioning eyes.

Epa looked down at his firstborn daughter who always seemed so beautifully calm and easy-going, with a mixture of joy, wondering and deep thoughts.

"I couldn't be prouder of you," he thought, as he recounted in his mind how Bailey had grown during the years. "I just hope I really showed you the right way to look at things."

He sighed.

"Somehow," he said to her, "We think that the 'least of these' means those that 'have the least.' The least amount of stuff. The least amount of food. The least cloth-ing. We think that having more is better."

He began to see another perspective from God; what the scriptures meant. He once again compared the privileges "back home," to the necessities of life in Africa. He considered the joy he saw in Mbarara, versus those who "had it all" in America.

There was a wide gap in spiritual satisfaction.

He was grateful he could give Bailey and Libby an education and a start in life they could work from. But somehow, it was here in Africa where the Barret family had found so much more than they ever thought possible; and from people—children—who had so little.

Epa stood up straight in the sunshine and looked into the crisp blue Ugandan sky. He was almost alone with his thoughts amid a sea of students, immensely enjoying the excited commotion he was hearing over something—bunk beds—that wouldn't create even a ripple in his reality in America.

"I can't even visit Uganda for a couple of weeks without three 50 pound bags of 'stuff' or return with fewer than one bag filled with dirty clothes," he said to Bailey still looking skyward. He shook and lowered his head. "I have way too much stuff. I couldn't do what these kids do everyday and do it with a joyful heart."

"I know what you mean," Bailey laughed thinking of her luggage full of fun snacks and foods, most of which she was giving away. "Me too! These children are so amazing. They are so thankful for so little."

"And we tend to elevate ourselves, somehow thinking we are 'more' than them," Epa said, looking at the kids laughing. "We have more stuff, so of course we must be better off. We can come to the developing world and give our 'stuff' to them."

He waved at some bunk beds going by, carried by PCM volunteers, with cheering children behind them.

"Most of this giving is out of abundance, our leftovers. It's what we don't need, no longer have or never even wear anymore. Because if we have 'more' we must be better, right?"

He looked down at her again, arm around her shoulder.

"Could it be that we really are the ones that are the 'least of these'? Us? The ones who 'have it all?'"

Bailey Barret hugged her Dad's arm and leaned on his shoulder.

"Thank you, Dad, for bringing us here," she said. "Thank you for following God, being obedient to Him and having the courage to think about these things."

She looked up at her father and smiled.

"I never get tired of coming here," she said. "I never will."

Chapter Twenty-Four

EPILOGUE: A REVELATION

"This is what life was meant to be, life the way He promised it would be if we followed Him, obeyed Him and just trusted. He will lead and guide us in the way we should go. We can do the things He has planned for us to do...if we would just trust Him."

—Mark Barret, Epa

"Jesus is the Beginning and the End, who loves us so much more than we know or realize."

—Monica Barret, Kiconco

"Life doesn't get any better than this," said Mark Barret after returning from Africa in June of 2011. Sitting in an East Texas burger restaurant in his home town, he calmly munched fries, cola and medium-rare beef. But Mark wasn't referring to the décor of the trendy burger place or his fully loaded hamburger.

Mark's mind was on a spiritual kingdom simultaneously far away and present in Spirit. His mental gaze was tuned east to the hospitality and humble love of Christians in lush, green Uganda. His heart was yearning for an experience with God he knew was happening, probably right now, that he was deprived of in America. An experience he wished he could somehow duplicate in his hometown but knew it could probably not be replicated the way it was happening in Mbarara.

"I mean," said Mark, returning to his french fries, "what more could I ask for? What more could I want? Hundreds of precious kids; Emmy and 'Supermom;' the dedicated staff, the full schools; God moving in their midst in such a powerful way; people giving it all to God and loving one another fully and doing it for real…Really, what else is there?"

The look in Mark's clear greenish brown eyes conveyed a conviction beyond syllables.

He thought of the honorary African names given to his family as a type of new identity, and induction into another reality: Kiconco, meaning "Gift of God" for Monica; Kyomu, "Precious" for Libby; Mbabazi "Kindness or Grace" for Bailey, and "Epa" for Mark—the shortened name of the Apostle Paul's friend in Philipppians 2.

Through his many trips to Africa, Epa encouraged everyone and anyone he knew to come and experience the awesome spiritual presence he had found at a humble school compound in Uganda. After an initial resistance to visiting Africa at all, Mark had become, to say the least, enthusiastic, as well as the entire family as they found "so much more."

"This is what life was meant to be," he said, nodding, "life the way He promised it would be if we followed Him, obeyed Him and just trusted that He will lead and guide us in the way we should go. We can do the things He has planned for us to do…if we would just trust Him."

Countless Christians would love to be able to say as Mark had, that life was full beyond description, that they were "living the dream" and could not conceive of having more. But many have turned away too soon from the realization of their dreams, as he'd nearly done himself.

Mark shook his head at the thought.

"And to think that I almost missed this," he said. "I mean, I'm 45 years old now. That's pretty late, but at least I know now. At least we get to do this now and hopefully for decades to come."

Mark knew he had nearly missed the family's moment, almost throwing aside God's vision for their lives as casually as one might toss a magazine on the floor. By his own account, responding to God's promptings and Monica's vision eventually yielded a blessing for the family beyond their own imaginations; far beyond financial and material plenty; far beyond living for themselves. They had all found that there really was so much more.

The physician was resistant to the whole idea at first, he admitted, because of two things.

"Life was good in Tyler, Texas," he said, "and Africa wasn't my own idea."

It was in peaceful and pastoral East Texas that Mark and Monica Barret and their daughters Bailey and Libby, Mbabazi and Kyomu, decided it was better to enter a world of poverty and the "underprivileged;" that it was better to ease the pain of those who could not even, in their wildest dreams, realize what they were missing in the Barret's reality—or in the reality of the average American.

And it was Christ that got underneath the shields of gold, penetrating any kind of "hands-off attitude" so many believers have—tugging at the heart and important matters of life.

In fact, it was the Barret children, Mbabazi and Kyomu, who came forward to gently prod their parents and courageously counsel their elders to claim a new identity in a world without frills; where fun was radically redefined as intense worship to the living God, "He who fills jars of clay" with treasure beyond description.

And when it came right down to it, Epa, Kiconco, Mbabazi and Kyomu were jars of clay, just waiting to be filled with treasure. Because they went, they were filled.

"The story started with Jesus, to tell the truth," said Kiconco, aka Monica.

"And that's the end of the story, too," she said. "Jesus is the Beginning and the End, who loves us so much more than we realize."

By the time Kyomu had designed the Christmas card with a missionary message at the "pushing" of Jesus, what was happening in the household was not odd at all. The spiritual seeds had been planted decades before in the faith experiences of Mark and Monica and were now sprouting at the right season, the right place and after all had been accomplished.

PCM USA proves that resources are necessary and appreciated in God's plan. Someone must amass, as the biblical Joseph did, and accumulate the resources needed to see the world through its spiritual and physical famine, at the proper time and precise moment.

This is the "Joseph model" Emmy Nnyanzi claimed as his own and "gave away his bitterness" so he could save his brothers as Joseph did. Jesus opened his eyes to those he could save—if he forgave.

This is the model Epa and Kiconco—Mark and Monica Barret have adopted, freely letting resources flow throw their fingers instead of tightly gripping what they own.

"My philosophy is not to have 'white knuckles' from holding on too hard, " said Mark sitting in his peaceful, country-decorated breakfast nook at home. "If God says 'give this up'" he said waving at his living room nearby, "then we give it up."

Such an attitude has brought manpower, materials and so much more to Uganda. Many volunteers have sacrificially "adopted" PCM as their own ministry. More volunteers are coming; new school grounds are being bought, bulldozed and built up into education and living centers.

What have Emmy and Sarah accomplished in the meantime with few material resources?

Perhaps of all society's "rejects" or "remaindered souls," orphans would be considered the most problematic; the most first suspected in incidents of vandalism; the ones most analysts would blame as the cause of school shootings, or even shootings in American churches or ministries.

Yet, this is not the character of the student population of PCM in Mbarara, Ibanda, Rwemikoma, Kyasenya or Minekye. Quite the opposite, Team 10 members from Texas discovered—as did all the previous and subsequent teams from the USA.

Emmy and Sarah have discovered more than forgiveness in Africa. So much more. They have discovered the path of living spiritual freedom, through the spiritual love of parental care.

God, it would appear, has seen fit that those most benefiting from Emmy and Sarah's courageous insight, with the help from Mark and Monica Barret's dedicated corps of volunteers, are those having the least power, position, pride and privilege in the eyes of the world. Friends from the West are privileged to visit PCM Uganda and dream that one day, they could live in a similar and remarkable spiritual reality—a place that Rocky Gill of Team 10 more than adequately described as "Heaven on Earth."

The End

HOW HE DID IT
A CONVERSATION WITH MARK BARRET

> *"The story of PCM is about how HE did it,*
> *not about how we did it."*

—Mark Barret

"Tenacious. Dedicated. All In. Won't quit. Won't let go. Trusting God in all things. These are qualities Mark brings to the USA side of Parental Care. They are qualities any ministry needs to have to fulfill the dreams and visions of where God is leading, Mark said.

That's because, as he freely admits, "At first, it's hard."

For every vision, purpose or task, a different set of strengths is needed. Parental Care is a successful ministry by many types of measuring; it's growing, people are coming to help; buildings are being built and money is coming in.

But the foundational success had always been there, in the fleshly building blocks of Emmy, Sarah, Mark and Monica who could hear God in the midst of poverty or pain, trial or testing, and trusted that God loved them, leading them every step of the way.

Talking things over with a cup of coffee in hand after Team 10 returned from Africa, Mark reflected on what he'd learned as a leader of a ministry that he thought at first, he couldn't do. He was asked to identify the elements that have made Parental Care a success.

"First you need to know God is calling you to do it," he said. "That's key. Sometimes you're not going to know right away. But eventually when you know He's calling you to do it, I think you just need to have some incredible endurance. Because at the beginning people are going to look at you like you're crazy. They're not going to totally think what you're doing or saying is legitimate. And they're not going to encourage you."

"They may say, "Well, how can you do it" or "You need to be involved in the church." But if the Lord tells you that "it's you" and that you're going to do it, then He's going to bring other people to be involved. You've got to be able to listen to who those people are, who will need to be with you."

"At first it's hard. I can't tell you how many nights I lay awake working, trying to organize the 120 kids in a form or fashion and present them as sponsorable early on. Seemingly unending questions present themselves. I had to think 'how are we going to show the kids; what are we going to do; how do we get the word out; who do we share with?'"

"Now I don't even have to show up to talk about it. Other people just want to talk about it constantly for us. That's what's so exciting for us, to see these great sponsors and supporters who are really captured by, and know what God is doing with, Emmy and Sarah.

As a physician you get a head start at the beginning because people will listen to you way before they will listen to other people. It was good to have a head start on that perspective. You have an instant platform on anything; people actually listen to you—most people, anyway."

Mark paused, then laughed.

"They don't always agree with you, but they'll listen. That's huge. It doesn't mean you have to be a doctor to do this; it means you have to have some kind of respectable position, at least getting a small core of people believing in the ministry. Then you've got to pray that somebody else comes and sees the vision you see."

"We knew God was calling us to do it. But when we started Parental Care in the United States, we were unsure we could do it. But the story of PCM is about how He, did it, not about how we did it."

"Emmy always said to us when we doubted, 'No, no, you can do it. The Lord will provide people for you.' We didn't quite believe that either. As we started praying, Jesus brought others alongside of us to help us and encourage us."

"So, you've got to have a calling; you've got have the endurance to hang in there, and don't listen to the discouragement of, 'Well, you're not with a church,' or 'No, we can't talk to you.'"

Starting Out

"The first group you talk to when you're starting out is kind of a humble group," Mark said. "But look, you've got to start somewhere.

"Emmy says, 'No, no, never despise a humble beginning,' and that is a big, big statement from him. He's lived it—and it's been true to what we are doing here. If the Lord tells you, 'put one brick' then put one brick. Then the second brick."

"Because when people see the truth, they are drawn to the ministry because of what God is doing, not what you're doing—it's what He's doing. You just get to bring people along. That's the fun part, because we have seen time and time again what the response has been. That they are blessed beyond imagination."

"The questions is, 'how do you get people over the initial fear, that certain fear factor, about traveling to the other side of the world and not being afraid to go; not being afraid of being stuck in the mud in the middle of nowhere? You just have to sort of say, 'Look, the Lord will take care of us.' The safest place to be is in the middle of God's will of what He's called you to do."

"A question people always ask is, 'Are you afraid when you go?' We should have a fear of the Lord and not a fear of anywhere He calls us to go."

"You've also got to have other people see the vision, at least a few, to say, 'This is real' and that will start something. If you go too long on your own, it can get tough. It was tough on us. I've been doing two jobs for three years. However, one of these jobs allows me to do the other one for nothing but the joy I receive in doing it. It's been the biggest blessing of my life to learn how to give, really give sacrificially."

"To be honest most of us are not going to work for a church. But all of us are going to have a job. We should all use our jobs to give what is already not ours back to the Kingdom of God to benefit others."

"Some people who knew me were saying "Well, what is he doing tonight?" They have no idea what it takes to communicate with leadership in Texas, leadership in Uganda, make decisions where capital goes, pray about what's next, where do we expand, contract, how do we add on staff?"

"Those are big decisions. I don't take them lightly. Sometimes you feel a little bit lonely, but I have some key friends that have been down roads like this before. Ministry friends such as Daniel Wallace. He has taught me to see truth better than any friend I have. He is a key friend. He is the one who said about the card Libby gave to Monica, 'Have you prayed about it yet?'"

"You don't need a lot of friends, but if you can pick a few good ones, ones that can teach you some important things, you will be blessed."

"Once you get started, you need at least one friend early to verbally tell you over and over "You are not crazy." It really helps if they will pray with you. I had such a friend in PCM Board member Les Jeske and I am forever grateful for this Christian brother. He was instrumental during the early days when there was so much to do and no one there to help."

"We think with this mind here, our own brains and our own thinking, that we have all the answers, but 1 Samuel 16:7 tells us, 'The Lord looks at the heart.'

"God is judging the heart. He wants to get to the heart, not to the mind. There is a disconnect when we start to solve things at the neck and above—we're going to fail."

"We call it supratentorial in medicine, and I'm including my mouth. It's as if we have 'brain to mouth' disease—it doesn't go into your heart."

"The heart has always been a big deal for me. That's really where I think people should be judged. That's the reason I feel my best friend is a Ugandan black man because I love his heart. We have a similar heart for the mission He's called us both to do and no matter what happens we are joined at the heart."

Money

"Your heart can get off track. One way to stay on track is to look at your checkbook. What do you do with what God is giving you? How are you spending time money and resources? If someone did a spiritual biopsy of you examining what have you done for God in the last two weeks, what would they find? If you're focused on the right thing, on the prize in Him, you can't really go wrong."

"If we let too many other things come in and be 'idols,' things that take up tons of time and using our resources on ourselves, it won't lead to anything. It's not necessarily bad by itself, but it just seems like we have so incredibly much here. Until you go see how people live on two dollars a day, well, you know it's true but you don't really know it."

"How one uses their resources is a reflection of where the heart is. Out of the heart the mouth speaks. It's the same thing. What are you saying? What are you doing with your time? What are you spending your time on? Add up all those things together and those are your influences. That's really a mini-reflection of you, to be honest. You can't just check in, punch the clock and go on. It's too superficial. It's not representative of what He wants us to do."

Figuring Out God's Will

"How do you know God's will? He's just going to confirm it through so many ways; through scripture, people and circumstances; through that peace when He talks to your heart, you're going to hear the message, you're going to hear him saying, 'You're going to do it. It's you. It's not going to be anyone else.'"

"Sometimes people come along that can thwart your effort as well, and if you don't see that, it can lead you to not doing what you've been called to. It's good to understand your weaknesses."

"God has called us all to do something for Him. There is a training ground, people have told us that, and we've seen that by being a part of different things—supporting missionaries and mission groups. He brings others around you then finally says, 'This is what I want you to do.' At least that's the way it was for us."

"We get to heaven by understanding what He did for us. Once we make it there I think He will ask us a couple of questions; 'How did you like my book, and what did you do for me?'"

Mark laughed.

"It's not a requirement to get in (to heaven), but I think there's going to be some sort of discussion. And if you don't know His book and what've you done for Him, what is your purpose being here? That's kind of simplified," he laughed again, "but you get the idea."

"It's easier to work in an organization when people are willing to learn. No organization is going to make all the right decisions, but if you are willing to learn and seek out good examples, that's a huge, huge blessing."

"It's like parenting. How do you learn to be good parents? Find good parents and spend time with them. It's the same thing with ministry; find a model of "doing it right, one with self-sustainment in mind and not just a handout. Find out who is doing it right and do what they're doing."

"You've got to have input from others to help make you grow, to make your ships head in the right direction. What surprised me the most was how easy it was to start a non-profit and then how little training so many people who are running them are getting."

"They are managing huge sums of money people are giving, and you can see how some of them go down from poor leadership or poor teaching. Where is the coaching involved? Where are the people taking small non-profit leaders, encouraging them, teaching them? It seems like you're on your own. You've got to be really aggressive on trying to find people to coach you.

"I have a 'non-profit coach' who asks me "Where does it hurt the most?" As a non-profit director, that's a great question. There are so many challenges, especially in this economy, because you have to keep growing or you're going to die."

"I say, 'Go where your heart is; really listen to what God is calling you to do; be realistic in your skill set and mind set, knowing 'I have these certain gifts and talents.' To help you in your weaknesses find people to assist you during that early transition when you and your wife are the whole staff as it was in our case."

Eternal Perspective

"When you figure out God's will, go 'all in.' It really is rare to see that, when people go 'all in' but the things we learn from people like that are powerful and important."

"People are hesitant to go all in because they are scared and afraid. They have a mindset of, 'this is the world I need to be worried about.' They don't have as much of an eternal perspective as they need. They can't get up high enough to see that all of this is going to go away, and it's not yours to begin with."

"That's question number one. Who does it belong to? Is it yours? Really? Or is it His? And if it's His, how much are you going to pay yourself to take care of something that's not yours?"

"I think the perspective is that we basically are resident aliens on this planet. We are called to be here, for a short time, a mere scratch in terms of eternity. We are given eight decades or so of life. How do we use that time? We need to be mindful that Eternity is forever. This is temporal. We can be gone tomorrow.

"I don't think it's God's chief goal for us to be happy in life. The purpose is to glorify Him in all that we do and say. Happiness comes from doing what He calls you to do and being obedient."

"There is SO MUCH MORE He is calling all of us to do."

The Real End

Web Extras: Check out this PCM Promo from 2010 and hear Pastor Emmy at http://www.youtube.com/watch?v=p4Cn8raleAA and a conversation with Mark and Monica Barret at http://www.youtube.com/watch?v=KB4IpoaAeWY

Made in the USA
San Bernardino, CA
19 November 2014